DISCOVERING
YOUR OWN DOCTOR WITHIN

AMY E. COLEMAN, MD

ISBN: 978-1-4834-4722-3 (sc)
ISBN: 978-1-4834-4721-6 (e)

Library of Congress Control Number: 2016902802

Lulu Publishing Services rev. date: 03/11/2016

Reviews of "Discovering Your Own Doctor Within"

"Here's a word visual for you: the way I see you is that you "operate" on these patients. There are no scalpels laid out or sutures at the ready, but it's surgery just the same. Your tools are carried within: all of your tuned listening and feeling sensors in order with your empathy and acceptance available in large supply. You may see a need to embrace an ailing heart, or clear blocked pathways obstructed by self-imposed limitations. Maybe you'll add a stent made of hope, or an implant of gratitude, or simply expose, remove or replace those programs that simply don't work. Whatever it is, you stand ready and available."

—Wellsmart "Doctor Within" Blog Subscriber

"With heartfelt stories, Dr. Amy Coleman shows you how she connects her patients to Love and God's presence where healing abides."

—Peggy Huddleston, author
Prepare for Surgery for Surgery, Heal Faster:
A Guide of Mind-Body Techniques

I'm really enjoying "Doctor Within." These are fantastic examples of spirituality, medicine, and psychology work together in people's lives. I can see your writing having a big impact on how physicians and other care providers administer care. Our culture is coming out of an era of seeing health as a one time surgery or check-up and antibiotics and is now seeing it as a whole way of living. If more, and maybe, one day, every physician saw health as a practice that incorporates mind, body, and spirit we wouldn't have to see these cases as breakthroughs. I'm looking forward to further reading.

—A Chaplain that worked at Cleveland Clinic

I haven't had a chance to thank you for sharing your manuscript. It came at the most opportune time. It and the messages in it were actually answers to some of my prayers! I really love it. What a rare doctor you are! I came across this workshop recently that reminded me of you (the whole body/

mind/spirit approach to healing) Are you familiar with Caroline Myss's work?

—Producer of Waking Heart Films

I've just completed reading through all of your recorded accounts and stand in awe of what you've accomplished here! You could not have sent this to me with any improved timing. It is the best gift you could ever have given me! I started to send an email your way, half way through reading these, but then found myself reading further and becoming immersed in what you share and how it speaks to me. I continue to marvel at all you bring, not just to me, but obviously to so many others. These stories yield everything from your sense of humor and ability to observe/read people with a direct/cut-to-the-chase approach, all the while disarming and dismantling false truths and replacing with restorative understanding, but also reveals your strength with uncovering, preserving, and exalting each person's unique value and beauty. It's your knowledge of, personal experience with, and simple explanation of these truths that we all need to apply to our lives that serves your patients so well; so life-saving. You know, I have always been fascinated with the challenges people face and the subsequent victories won in their lives; to see/understand what is/ was needed to overcome personal challenges. This story collection is a presentation of these challenges; our ailments, expressed self limitation, fear, threat, regret, and self worth issues .....all met head on with your empathy, understanding, a bright light to expose the real source of trouble, and an arsenal of salves and healing truths to repair and resurrect. You've captured these experiences beautifully! This is golden stuff. I see in you this tremendous efficiency of thought, time, action with all things. Such clarity; distillation...is more accurate the word to assign. I attribute this to you being in concert with God's intentions for you and those around you. I'm envious.

—Former patient and engineer for a Fortune 500 Company

DEDICATION

This book is dedicated to all my patients, who teach me more than could ever be learned from formal education.

To my mother, who instilled within me the courage to speak my truth. To my father, for his endless support.

To the Flag Officers of the U.S. Air Force: Gen. William T. Hobbins (Ret.), Gen. Roger Brady (Ret.), MGen. Jack Briggs and medical officer John Mace (Ret.) who all ordered and encouraged me to carry confidently on with the type of healthcare I offer, and the message within it.

To all the young physicians that question how to exist as their best self within the demands of the current ailing healthcare system, I dedicate this book.

"When we live the vision of what we want to see from within despite having no current model of physical evidence which supports it, we will change the world by changing ourselves first, and the world will soon follow."

—AEC

CONTENTS

When we see the nature of us as being well, and the power of our thoughts to produce reality, only then are we ready to begin to understand the nature of disease versus wellness.

—Amy E. Coleman, MD

INTRODUCTION

I've always been attracted to journals, with their beautifully bound, blank pages. I must own at least ten of them, most untouched. When I enter a bookstore, the journals are my first stop. Despite all the authors' works lining shelves in front of me, with beautiful glossy covers and eye-catching names, I'm drawn to the empty void of the unlined journal. Just recently I was reminded of why: standing in an aisle of a particularly beautiful selection of Italian leather–bound blank journals, I whispered to myself, "I have a story to tell." This impulse came to me as a chill up and down my spine, which, over the last several years, I've come to understand is a sign that what I'm thinking at the moment of that feeling means I'm on the right track. A warm fuzzy such as this speaks volumes, just as butterflies in the stomach or a lump in the throat do.

I wasn't always enamored with personalizing blank books off of a bookstore shelf. I used to make my own. As a child, I folded neat piles of printer paper down the middle, stapled them all together, and then filled the bundle with all the information and illustrations about my pets, birds seen on bird-watching trips, or other subjects that were important to me. As an adolescent, I captured vacations, fitness-training regimens, and the lessons I learned in training sessions with my horse.

Now, as an adult, I feel pulled toward recording instances of my life that reflect the change in perception I've experienced since 2006. This was the year when I prayed earnestly to be led toward answers to the real workings of the world. Since then, I have been blessed by consciously receiving answers during prayer and meditation. I also receive insight after dreams that relay a lesson or meaning upon waking, which I then capture by jotting down in a journal or notepad. I receive wisdom everywhere because I've asked for it and continue to actively listen for it. Sometimes it's in the form of a book or introspective moment that contains just the answer to the question I had in mind. I'm blessed with all the information and experience I can possibly handle. It continues to this day and will never be complete.

The following stories of patient encounters are a first attempt to outline how I'm applying the information I have received in the day-to-day visits with my patients. These most recent patient encounters take place at a regular clinic, where I do work as an independently contracting family medicine physician. The clinics are: occupational medicine, wellness/preventative clinics, family medicine, and/or urgent care, with minor trauma-care capabilities. My writing, like my patient encounters, seems to take on a life of its own at times, but I'm glad to put my fingers on the keyboard and give this task of recording these memories the effort it deserves.

In residency, a faculty member was describing me to a fellow colleague and said, "You know, she's the one who is nice to her patients."

How could I be otherwise? I've been a patient myself. And what's more, as an Air Force flight surgeon, for five years I was intricately woven into my patients' lives in the military, with a deeply felt connection to my troops that made all the difference. I trusted them to bring me back safely after missions, and they trusted me to always be attuned. Returning from the military and then going into an academic setting, I found that this depth of interconnectedness is not well understood. A separation is placed between doctor and patient, and so I'm here as a testimony that this space need not exist.

Doctors use a snap judgment process with patients that starts in the brain and, as a result, is always short-sighted and lacking. Pilots, on the other hand, make snap judgments but instead use their gut or instinct. The benefit is that the gut always acts in the moment and so operates as a proper tool for immediate perception; however, the highest level of snap judgment we can make is through our hearts. When we walk in with open hearts, the real lay of the land is made known to us. Seeing through the eyes of love not only opens awareness to what is but also dissolves self-protective mechanisms held by both the doctor *and* the patient. Meeting in this space creates a new realm of true potential. When the more well-known, conventional means are used in the doctor–patient encounter, then only a small array of potential solutions are available.

The irony in this type of encounter is that it may look completely the same as the other type of encounters with similar, if not identical, patient records or notes generated. The difference lies in the unseen: a formidable, empathic connection is formed, from which full potential is possible. In upholding this balance within a patient encounter, you remind them of the possibility of nonjudgment and heartfelt awareness, or emotional intelligence, and if they choose, they may begin to apply it in their own lives. After all, the strongest teaching example is in being what you teach!

Armed with new skills by which to see the world, patients now have new keys to the locked vaults in their lives and a crucial, lasting reminder of their potential for wellness. Fostering patient relationships in this way directs them to their own doctor within.

CHAPTER 1

The Power of Prayer

A Death Wish

An angry young man in his early twenties sat on the table and began to tell me how stupid he thought this appointment was. The reason for his visit was an annual hearing test deemed mandatory by his employer. He complained that it made no sense to come in every year and be seen by a physician simply to have his audiogram results signed in order to go back to what he really needed to be doing: his work. He stated emphatically that he'd never seen a doctor for more than just a few minutes about anything and the encounters had always been brusque and rude.

When I asked about his medical history, he informed me that he'd had a heart attack at the age of twenty-six. Going further, he said he was told at the hospital that when he drank alcohol, his blood became thicker. They went on to tell him that this caused a clot to form and that he would need a multi-vessel bypass. He added that he still drank when he wanted to because "everyone has to die some time."

I sat and listened. When I asked why he was so angry, he began to list the instances in his life that had been unfair to him, including the death of his sister, a divorce, bankruptcy, the death of his parents and mother-in-law from cancer, a recent eviction, and so on. His countenance was one of fear, and when I presented this to him gently, he made sure I knew that we did not and would not see eye to eye. To him, this visit was another waste of time. Despite this, he remained on the exam table, although I had expected him to walk out.

I told him, "Your beliefs are not the truth." Then I continued: "When I don't know what's going to help someone, prayer always seems to work."

I asked him if I could pray for him, and he sullenly agreed. (He'd just finished telling me that he didn't believe in anything.) At that time, my heart went out to this troubled fellow. I prayed for God to give this gentleman all of the grace that God had given me, as he felt like a brother to me. I prayed that he would have guidance, and all the help he needed to find his way to what he truly wanted. I prayed for his protection and insight, for all beliefs that did not serve him to fall away, and for his health to be restored.

When I was finished, the patient was noticeably approachable and relaxed. He apologized for the time he took. I let him know, in complete honesty, that he was a true blessing to me that day and that I was thankful he had come in. Before he was discharged, he even asked if I had a business card. His countenance was even-keeled, almost as if he had just gotten up from a nap, and his anger had vanished.

A Tearful Anniversary

A patient had come in for a truck driver's medical card, or DOT exam, for the Department of Transportation. He was an older man with a very round belly and a boylike face that was narrow for his body type, and behind the wrinkles, he had bright blue eyes. He was a talker, so I just sat and listened.

He mentioned that today was the one-year anniversary of his father's death. He recalled that his father had passed away in a chair from a very quick, large stroke shortly after he'd retired from truck driving. Though he had been seemingly dedicated to trucking, one day after a delivery his father simply "hung it all up" with no notice and with no previous indication that he was going to retire. This patient then described how his father pined for lost relatives, telling stories of his grandpa, who was also a trucker in his day. After the patient had delivered many stories about his family of truck drivers with a straight face and smile, he then developed a quiver in his bottom lip and cried, "I miss my dad." He bowed his head and sobbed, shoulders heaving with every shaky breath. I comforted him and let him know that every time he felt love for his father and remembered all his wonderful memories, they were reunited.

The patient agreed and told me a story he'd not told anyone, since "no one wants to flaunt their Christianity, and they would think I was crazy." He told me that something had happened to him while sitting in the pew at his grandfather's funeral. Not having known whether the newly departed family member had been saved, he sat quietly with his head bowed and said, "Lord, I hope that he is up there." Then came the response in his ear; it was a voice that sounded direct yet gentle, and it said clearly, "Don't worry; he is with me."

I let the patient know that we are souls, or part spirit, ourselves. So we really aren't as separated as we think from the spirits of our loved ones. I gave him a hug and told him to fully enjoy the day with his dad today. I encouraged him to talk with him. The patient apologized for taking so much time but thanked me as well, saying, "God bless you. God bless you for your patience and your listening."

A Caring Heart

Another patient, as in the previous story, came in for a DOT examination. He too had been a trucker for most of his life, and he was still going strong despite a recent five-vessel heart-bypass surgery. He spoke about caring for the environment, and he had been very concerned about stopping at a truck stop with a fellow trucker who had hauled a piece of machinery that cut down the rainforest at a speed that took the place of seventeen hundred men. He shook his head in disbelief as he described it as "a bush hog for trees." He also spoke to me about his love of animals and how he never hunted or fished, and rarely ate meat other than fish or chicken. I supported his efforts toward a vegetarian diet—a diet to which I also adhere. I asked him how we could help other people to see that they could make a difference when it comes to the environment. He answered that most people don't think that it affects them, because it doesn't appear to impact them directly, so they "don't care and turn a blind eye." He then added wisely, "Everything has a purpose for existing, even the smallest creature, and we must respect that. People just don't care enough."

I agreed and added that we're all made of the same stuff from God, so we must all be related and must care about each and every creature and person. Astonished, the patient said that he hadn't felt comfortable sharing his views for fear of being judged; he went on to say that he planned to keep our conversation as a special memory. He further disclosed that he was married to a person who held none of the same beliefs, and so he'd learned to keep his opinions to himself. I told him that he takes everything to heart. He nodded in agreement when I asked if this is what had happened to his heart to cause the need for the bypass.

Interestingly, when he was receiving the heart bypass, the patient mentioned that he'd begun to feel himself drift toward a tunnel, consciously aware of a light that resembled a circular, brilliantly white mist that came nearer and nearer. Just as he was putting his arms out to meet it, the light snapped shut and was no more. The patient said he was standing in the darkest dark he had ever experienced, and yet he felt a presence there with him. This frightened him so much that he thought he was in hell! At this point he began to regain consciousness, and the event became a memory. He tried to tell this story later, but it was discounted and discredited by others as a dream. He relayed to me that it was not a dream but a true experience that he didn't understand to that day.

I explained to him that near-death experiences are very well documented and seem to point toward the same truth. I mentioned that dying was as easy as getting up from one chair and sitting down into another. The spirit lifts from the shell of the body and rejoins the world of spirit from which it came. While in transition, there are those on the other side of the physical realm who have known and loved you enough to come and watch over your passing; many times they are loved ones who have passed before you. They assist with any disorientation that one may feel during this process so that you're never alone. In addition to being documented in episodes of near-death experiences, others who have been hypnotized and have experienced past-life events have identical stories. The patient was relieved that what he had felt had happened was indeed true.

He also mentioned that when he felt frightened, he was able to pull in energy and re-center with a prayer. I told him that was exactly what science was on the cusp of proving now. The fields of torsional physics, plasma physics, and quantum physics are developing theories about how energy can create a vortex of potential within you. The degree of how centered and powerful this spin is depends on what thoughts or intentions it was made of. Empathy, or love, is a frequency that is able to become very dense and spin very fast without toppling or becoming unbalanced. In nature and love, there is no destructive interference. With other, less lofty thoughts, such as guilt or despair, our centers of spin become unbalanced and topple over like a top that has been put on a crooked path:one that has has lost its momentum and is trying to remain upright for a moment more. Everything, I explained, is created from positively and negatively charged particles. This includes everything we are made of at the most basic atomic level. This made a lot of sense to the patient and helped explain to him as to how prayer and deep breathing were so helpful. After the patient passed his physical, I thanked him for being a gift to me that day by coming in. I truly felt blessed in the company of this man and encouraged him to spread his insight, trusting that he would find the right people with which to share this information.

The Workaholic

This patient had arrived for a problem with fatigue during a bout of bronchitis that had not been getting better. When I walked into the room, I was hit directly with the smell of cigarette smoke. In the chair by the exam room table sat a man in his early fifties. He was scruffy but well kept, with very dark circles under his eyes and a sallow, blotchy complexion. He was direct, brash, and no-nonsense. He wanted to be better as of yesterday, but his fatigue and upper respiratory trouble would not abate. When I asked how much he smoked, this patient replied, "Not enough." He then admitted to smoking one and a half packs a day and briefly described that he had difficulty with depression.

As I examined him, I felt that he put up an emotional wall, and he seemed to enjoy making sidebar remarks that, while humorous, were biting and distrustful from a deeper level. His physical exam was nondescript and basically normal. His lungs were clear, and there was no infection in the ears or throat. His abdomen had hyperactive bowel sounds, and his liver was tight and firm. He had no swollen lymph nodes, which would've indicated mononucleosis, and his spleen was normal, which also could've been swollen as a result of the virus.

From lessons I'd learned in acupuncture and Chinese medicine, his blotchy complexion and physical findings suggested what seemed to be a rising "liver fire." This meant he got angry and stayed angry for long periods of time. When I asked him if this was the case, he admitted he did. The gentleman went on to discuss how he often skipped meals during his hard shift work. He was also taking care of his school-age son, and only got three hours of sleep a night because his mind "was going a hundred miles an hour." He denied drinking alcohol or using drugs. To make sure he was not in any physical danger from infection or illness, an x-ray was performed and a monospot test was done to rule out mononucleosis. Both were negative for serious disease.

The x-ray, while without pneumonia, tuberculosis, or a collapsed lung, still had a story to tell. There was a subtle message that I prayed my eyes would unveil: the bronchi were inflamed, and the lungs looked to be very mildly enlarged on both sides. This could've meant that he was in the early stages of COPD, or chronic obstructive pulmonary disorder. From the looks of the bronchi, he also could've been suffering from chronic bronchitis, most assuredly from smoking so much.

Before I reentered the room from reading the x-ray, I said a prayer that I might be able to love this man enough to truly help him, and I asked for help from above. I cleared my mind and entered, feeling the patient's vulnerability in waiting for the news I was about to give him. I first started with the good news: no mass, no pneumonia, and no collapse. I then told him about the subtle variations that were painting a picture of long-term neglect and abuse of the lung from smoking and from him not taking care of himself. I drew a picture of his lung as slightly overinflated, which meant less elasticity and made moving air more difficult for the lung. A lung without good tissue elasticity is akin to a flimsy plastic grocery bag; it cannot squeeze the air out or bring it in effectively. Conversely, a healthy lung with firm tissue tone is like a bellows.

Coincidentally, he mentioned that his friend had just talked to him about COPD. At that point, I decided that tough love was needed. I asked him how he expected his body to get better in good time on three hours of sleep, infrequent meals, and a diet of cigarettes and coffee. Further, I'd inquired as to why he didn't love himself enough to take care of his body. He look startled but amused and quipped that I didn't have enough time for his whole story. When I encouraged him, "Try me," he shared a piece of helpful information.

He'd been working fifteen-hour days during his career for a long time. His marriage had suffered, but he was unaware of this until he'd walked in on his wife cheating on him. He told me that he had felt annihilated, as he'd loved his wife very much and would never have cheated on her. Having had forgiven his wife and since moved on, he understood why the cheating had occurred and realized they truly had had no relationship thanks to the hours he'd kept at work. Over time, he'd put himself through all the help books he could find, but none of them had worked.

Einstein once stated that it's easy to see from an objective point of view how no one can fix a problem from the same level that it's occurring. To see the larger picture is paramount, which requires us to "get above the weeds," or rise above the situation. With that in mind, I asked this patient if he had any spirituality to his life. He replied that he believed in nothing of the sort; "we're here and then we die" was his mantra.

Beside where I'd sketched a picture of his lungs, I doodled a triangle. Each leg, I'd explained, is a component of what keeps us balanced. One leg is the physical, one is the mental, and one is the spiritual. I told him that we all have a soul that is our spiritual side, and when this is ignored, it puts too much work and pressure on the mind to sort out big-picture details of life, which the mind is unable to do. This is what sets the mind to race and causes symptoms of depression. I then went on to explain that no church or organized religion was needed. "Spirituality can be thought of as getting in touch with our highest, best self. Others take example from those who showed the way before, such as Jesus, Buddha, or Krishna. All of these point the way to the fact that we're all more than the physical."

I knew right then that I had to get my point across to that man; I saw a small yellow light that glowed behind his right shoulder, and so I knew he was there for this purpose: to seek help onto the path beyond what existed daily for him. As an aside, patients have presented to me with these lights behind them for years. I've come to know that these are their guardian angels who need assistance with moving the person toward more spiritual understanding. At the very least I could be a sensible, caring voice of concern for an individual. Each person has a slightly different color of light, along with a lesser or greater intensity, accompanying him or her. Most lights just flash for a moment and then are gone, as if to say, "I am here."

For this patient, in a particular instant when the light flashed, I felt the word *sister* arise in my mind but didn't share that with the patient, so as to not to startle him. That, and I didn't want to distract him from what we were there to discuss. Had his sister died traumatically, it would've kept him focusing on that moment. Instead, I told him that someone loved him enough to bring him in that day so he could hear what he needed to hear and get onto a better path. I explained briefly about the lights and that he had one over his shoulder. I said it was more than coincidence that he'd heard about COPD from his friend and then from me in such a short interval of time. His mind had been trying to correct itself but was too close to the problem to be effective at rescuing itself. I perceived that he'd forgiven his wife yet had not forgiven himself. During that time, his countenance became rosier, and I saw that he truly had a big heart. The bags under his eyes then seemed much less dark. I told him he was an amazing person with a big heart and gave him a big hug.

To lighten up the situation, I then went back to a purely physical focus. I discussed that I'd give him an antibiotic to help with any secondary bacterial infection from the five weeks of bronchitis. We often treat smokers with antibiotics, as they're more prone to develop pneumonias. I also recommended that he quit smoking. He expressed interest in Chantix, a smoking-cessation drug, and I was overjoyed. It was all the invitation I needed to write up a prescription for the entire course. Then the patient asked me if this would make him better. I told him, in complete seriousness and sincerity, that it might help him get better but that he would not stay better until he addressed the real needs we'd discussed.

"Life is a hell and then you die," he told me.

I replied, "If I was seeing life through the same perspective that you choose to see it, I would think I was in hell too." I then asked if I could pray for him or if he would rather me pray after he left.

He said, "If you feel like you need to pray, you should go ahead and pray."

I considered this an invitation and placed one hand on his forearm and bowed my head. I prayed that he would be guided toward health and a sense of what is the truth. I prayed that he would release the walls that bound and held him from this and that he'd have all the share of grace with which God had blessed me. I prayed for the safety of his son and thanked God for the lessons in virtue that children bring: joy, love, and patience in a time in our lives when it's all too easy to believe in the illusion of cynicism.

As usually happens when I pray, tears welled, and I let them fall on the sleeve of my sweater. At the conclusion of the prayer, I didn't immediately look directly at the patient but felt and saw from the corner of my eye his head down. He seemed a bit stunned. I grabbed a tissue behind me and invited the patient to walk his chart to the checkout desk whenever he was ready. He sat for a while in his seat after I left before leaving the room to check out and go pick up his son.

An Actress Within

A girl in her midtwenties who wore a peasant shirt arrived for a simple checkup of her sprained right wrist. She'd been wearing a brace and managing within her work restrictions. Blonde-haired and doe-eyed, she appeared reserved but polite. I proceeded to examine the wrist and check the fit of the brace. I also offered her a different medication and asked about physical therapy. We then chitchatted a bit, during which she told me she was working an assembly line job and raising her sons, but she'd just graduated from acting school and was very excited to audition the next day for a commercial in Cincinnati. She thought it was important to show her sons the importance of following a dream by following her own. She said she'd always wanted to portray characters that brought out emotions in those watching. I commended her for this and wished her the best for the audition. I encouraged her to show the joy in what she was doing, even if it was an awkward tryout, as though the time on stage would truly be what she'd be doing for a living; projecting her comfort would allow the producers to feel more relaxed and happy to hire her for the part. I asked her if there was anything else about her health that we should talk about, and she stated she'd had migraines since childhood.

I felt a sense of properness while in the room with her; a sense of calmness that was more like forced tranquility than genuine peace. So, I brought to her attention that allowing her true feelings to come out, such as anger, would not only help with her migraines but also with her performance on stage. I felt that somewhere during this young adult's upbringing, she'd learned to turn off any anger, having judged and condemned it as improper.

"As a matter of fact," I told her, "anger can be very helpful."

I recommended that she join a self-defense class where she could strike out, kick, and punch, and with each one of these offensive moves, assign with it something that happened to her that caused her to feel angry. She was to channel that feeling and event into every strike.

I told her that if she did that, she would not only help her migraines but also be able to channel that emotion in the human characters she played. I explained that the suppression of this emotion doesn't get rid of it but instead just chains it up for a while and builds inner pressure that can result in all sorts of destructive influence on the body. Emotions are vibrations, and the body, under poor vibrations, can develop disease and be unwell, exhibiting symptoms such as migraines, ulcers, and stomach issues.

She nodded in agreement and said that in her final exam at acting school, she'd had to deliver part of a monologue of a very angry woman, standing alone on stage. She said she had done very poorly because she hadn't been able to get in touch with the anger. I'd told her that it made a lot of sense because she'd never given herself permission to access it. While she worked through this, I recommended that she try butterbur, an herb showing promise in treating migraines, embraced by large neurology clinics for its effectiveness and low side effect profile.

I then asked if I could say a prayer with her for her audition and new dream career. She agreed, and I held in my mind the portrait of her as an actress who was so in touch with each of her emotions that she could portray any character, and the genuineness of this would be felt by all the audience members, who would be in turn inspired to find the genuine nature in their own lives. I saw this so clearly for her and asked that she be guided to this, as she felt comfortable in allowing it to happen. She'd been an inspiration, and I was blessed with a new realization about prayer from our visit.

In having prayed and seen the young actress so sharply in my mind's eye doing and loving what she wanted so much to do, I felt what true prayer is. True prayer is holding a deeply felt,detailed image of someone's best self, when he or she isn't yet able to do so. I was reminded of Jesus among the sick. He saw his fellow beings in their full state of radiant health, walking with their beds instead of focusing on their lameness and skin lesions. He held so strongly the vibration of their well-being that they all let go of their own beliefs of sickness in his presence. We can all do this for each other by focusing on each other's best selves and holding that in our hearts as our image of them.

CHAPTER 2

The Hidden Psychology

The Human Hurricane

"Did you come packing?" he asked when I walked into the room. A man in his sixties with gray hair and expressive eyes was sitting on the exam room table. He had a large frame and was built like a lumberjack.

I shook his hand and introduced myself and then placed my other hand on the patient's shoulder. "There's no need for guns here," I said warmly. The patient was referring to the drama he'd caused at his last visit to the clinic.

At the time of the ruckus, I was seeing a patient who was this man's employee. As I heard raised voices outside the door during the trouble, my patient had shaken his head and said, "That's my boss. He can be a loose cannon sometimes."

When I came out of the room that day, my colleague, Dr. L, was as white as a sheet and visibly shaken. She began to tell me how this gentleman, who wanted to secure a medical certification in order to drive commercially for his self-owned trucking business, had for years failed to follow up with his cardiologist to book a checkup after receiving stents in his heart. This meant the patient was disqualified for truck driving and hadn't been given a pass on his exam until he returned to his cardiologist for clearance.

My colleague recounted that the patient, upon hearing this, had strode strongly up to the doctor, grabbed the paperwork in front of her, crumpled it up, and thrown it to the ground. Dr. L had become very fearful and had immediately walked out of the room and reported the situation to the technicians, stating emphatically that she would not enter the room again under any circumstance. She said she would never see him again and wrote a report of the problem in the patient's chart. She feared that he might hit her. The patient left soon after the incident and was to come back after seeing his cardiologist.

When the patient had returned to clinic, the front staff were immediately on alert. The tension had been palpable. The patient himself felt fearful after his previous behavior, and so did the staff. The front desk clerk had come to me and stated that they hadn't yet received the patient's stress test report from the cardiologist's office, and they feared that the extra wait would drive up the man's blood pressure enough that he would fail for yet another reason: hypertension. There had been a feeling of awkwardness in the clinic, and a physician's assistant sitting beside me in the back of the clinic at a common workstation asked me, "Do you want me to see him?"

"No," I said politely. "It isn't the loud, boisterous ones that you have to worry about. With these people, you always know where you stand. It is the silent, brooding ones that will one day explode without any ability to control it at that point. Those are the truly dangerous."

When the fax had finally arrived from the cardiologist's office, the front office staff passed it to me, along with all of the patient's paperwork, including his DOT physical, though it was only half complete due to the mishap with Dr. L. I'd then taken a deep breath and said a prayer that I would be able to see this man as God sees him and be able to truly help.

In the room with the patient, I was centered and calm, feeling warmness toward this man as I shook his hand. I sensed him relax when I smiled at him. He had plenty to say, yet he started with an apology about how he'd treated the other doctor. He said he'd known she was scared, because he'd seen fear in her eyes, and that made him feel very bad. He'd been so frustrated because no one had told him he was supposed to go to see the cardiologist. When he'd asked questions about how to stay within the DOT guidelines, he was told only to go to the website.

At this point he admitted that he'd never learned how to use a computer. To make matters worse, he'd never finished high school and was dyslexic. He told me that he'd overcome this with will and determination and had started his own successful trucking company, paying off in cash all of his large truck purchases thanks to his profits. He'd also told the story that he'd always made his requirements plain to his employees so they'd always known where they stood. When it came to DOT, he said that there seemed to be no way to win, and he never knew the rules or where to find them.

I agreed with the patient on this. If a patient wasn't savvy, he could easily be swept up in the system, dazed and confused about what to do next when he had a health problem that required several steps to become recertified to drive. The patient went on to say that the last interaction with Dr. L hadn't started off well. He'd sensed when the doctor had come in that she was a bit defensive. When he'd asked about what he needed to do to get back to driving, the doctor had stated the requirements and told him he could reference this on the website. When he'd said he didn't use computers, he felt what he perceived as the doctor belittling him or looking down on him, which had thrown him into a fury. He stated that he never stood for someone looking down on him and that his whole life was a story of success by getting beyond that feeling. Lastly, the patient told me that the past several months had been very hard due to the impending divorce from his wife of thirty-seven years, who had decided that it was time to leave.

When it was my turn to talk, I began to paint a picture for this gentleman. I started with calling his attention to the fact that he had a large personality. You could truly feel the magnetism about him that both wanted to care for others and be acknowledged. "You create the weather around you, and I don't mean sunshine or rain," I said, speaking figuratively to acknowledge the fact that this man, wherever he went, drew attention to his presence and could use that in a very productive way by shining humor and joy or sending everyone into a tornado of anxiety. He created a real atmosphere that all depended on his own state at the time.

"People are a mirror to your own state of mind," I continued. "Right now, you're seeing the result all around you that you are not as healthy emotionally as you need to be. The evidence of this flies back in your face from seeing all the calamity of others interacting with you."

He nodded in agreement and added that when he was happy, people flocked to his side just to talk to him and be near him. I went on to explain that he'd just lost the security net of a loving home with his wife, and that this had truly shocked his sense of being okay. It had brought out his insecurities and his need to defend himself, just as he had done with Dr. L.

"No one can make you feel inferior or belittled unless you are truly feeling a bit of that within you already," I said. "During a divorce, it's only natural that these feelings come up."

I then sat beside the patient on the exam room table and introduced the idea that we have three parts to ourselves: the mind, the body, and the soul. The body represents the employees, with each cell working daily to produce everything the industry of you needs. The mind is the manager and the spirit, or soul, is the CEO. I explained that if any manager is given the role of CEO, it's always too much responsibility. Likewise, if we aren't aligned with our spirit or soul, the mind begins to try and fill in the responsibilities of keeping it all together. The problem is that the mind doesn't have the vision to do so, and it then becomes more and more anxious, thinking at a hundred miles an hour or more, to attempt to fill in all the cracks of perceived lack, worry, and strain.

The mind then becomes a terrible boss, creating an atmosphere of complete tension and overwork for all of the body's cells. Instead, if the soul or spirit is in alignment through prayer or meditation, we realize that our truest strength is then plugged into our daily tasks and the mind can relax and function as it should.

I asked the patient if he practiced any form of spirituality, and he replied that he did, but not actively. I went on to explain that it need not be a religion of any kind, or an active process such as going to church, but that we were made in the image of God, which is true spirit, and we can come into contact with that at any time just by holding the thought of that in a moment of stillness and intend for knowing this part of us.

I then asked if I might say a prayer with him, and he was glad to participate. As I held his hand, I thanked the Lord for his purpose in this life and his gifts and asked that he'd feel a greater sense of strength during this challenging time. The prayer had progressed for a few minutes and then ended with a hug. Both of us were tearful but experienced a state of appreciation and peace. He then left the clinic without incident, along with the necessary clearance to drive his truck commercially. The entire clinic had held its collective breath as he walked out, but there was no resistance left in him, only peace and quiet.

The technician came back to me and asked if I'd spent all that time in there with him. When I answered yes, she said, "We were all worried about you and were going to knock on the door to make sure you were okay."

I told her that there had been no need but thanked her all the same. She said that she'd noticed that his complexion was no longer red-faced and that he'd looked very peaceful and calm—so much so that she'd barely recognized him when he'd left.

The true lesson had finally surfaced. Only you have the responsibility of sorting yourself out. Then, the reflection of that will be seen as an ease and allowance of what you want to happen naturally.

This Medicine Isn't Working, Doc!

A patient I hadn't seen before came in for a follow-up appointment after receiving testosterone injections. He'd been receiving intramuscular shots of testosterone for the last three weeks from a colleague of mine, and he was plain in his concern: that the shots hadn't worked. He still felt tired and had low libido. Since he was in the midst of another physician's care, I was picking up on a conversation already in progress and so offered education first: why hormones are so slow to act.

Most medicines we use for an energy boost, like vitamin B12, go directly into the bloodstream and have the ability to enter directly into cells as their active component, stimulating whatever effect it has on the body without delay. Hormones, on the other hand, are encoded clumps of information that the cell must first bring into its nucleus, which is the central processing unit, much like a computer's motherboard. From here, the cell breaks down the code of the hormone and then transcribes it into DNA. From this, the DNA is used to generate a protein that creates the actual usable hormone for the cell. This goes for all hormones generated by the body, such as the thyroid hormone, estrogen, prednisone, testosterone, and so on. This is why thyroid levels in people being treated with medicine change so slowly and also why women have monthly cycles instead of daily menstruation cycles. From this I explained to him that his testosterone levels had probably just begun to rise and that it would take some time to notice any changes.

The patient seemed interested to know that it was pretty normal for these levels to take a while in turning around; however, I explained to him that the deeper processes of the body prefer to use certain hormones over others depending on a person's perceived stress level. (I said "perceived" because anything can happen to a person, and if they have no emotional upset or resistance about it, there will be no perceived stress by the body.)

I then explained that the body's pathway of using testosterone is based on whether the body is ready to engage in sexual activity. A body that's ready is in a state of wellness, with no perceived threat. Threat is stress, and stress creates a need for the body to reach for the stress hormone instead of the sex hormone for its well-being. In fact, both hormones, testosterone and stress, come off of the same assembly line. So, the increased production of one slows production of the other. A body in perceived stress will turn off the production of testosterone in favor of the production of the stress hormone, just like a person running from a bear creates more adrenaline than digestive juices. The body knows what's needed by perceiving the underlying emotional vibration. After all, on the microscopic level, we really are vibrations of charged energy at our most fundamental unit.

In this man I felt a sense of determination and will, yet also sheer fatigue from the strain of it all. Being in the same room with him was the same sensation as when you walk into a kitchen and see a pressure cooker, working away on the stove. There is some sense of trepidation there, with a feeling of tension and intensity in it's presence. I described this to him and then gave him the comparison of someone more like a crock pot, cooking away in the corner. This I described as a warm, inviting presence, slow and nonthreatening—not even noticeable cooking away in the corner until you smell the heavenly fragrance of its work. This teaches us that there are two ways to do a job. To show the first way, I gritted my teeth, clenched my fists, closed my eyes, contorting my face in tension, and declared: *"I am going to cook this food!"* To demonstrate the second way, I then loosened up and swayed back and forth, speaking musically with a happy smile on my face: "I am going to cooook this foooood."

I continued with this analogy by saying that we can approach our job either as a pressure cooker or a crock pot because the choice is always up to us; however, the decision becomes the action the body takes to try and support you in your choice. If you act like a pacing tiger in a cage, you'll always need more stress hormone, and your sex hormone will naturally diminish. At that moment the patient gave a look of complete identification to the metaphor and said, "I feel that my cage is getting smaller all the time."

Here was the conundrum. The patient, from outside perceived obligations and expectations, had whittled down his feeling of freedom to a small cage that was getting smaller.

"Sounds very familiar," I said, and I called his attention to the fact that there were several other patients waiting that day. In the current atmosphere of medical care run by insurance companies, doctors were encouraged to see more patients per hour, invariably pushing performance over quality every day in our offices. I explained that many doctors tried to keep up with the demands upon them by moving faster, harder, and with greater urgency.

I asked him what his past visits were like, and he related briefly that he was never with the doctor for more than two to five minutes. I then asked him if, in taking more time, I had been doing a worse job. His response was, "No, not at all! The contrary!" I then told him that if I could create time for the job to be done right, he could too; it was all a matter of perspective. The patient then nodded in agreement.

At this point I asked him to pursue a measure of connection to nature that would show him how to slow down and enjoy each moment. All that was needed was to simply walk in nature and share time with animals. I told him that our most powerful point of creation is in the present moment, and in order to be aware of that moment, we must slow down our mind's chatter and change our perception. Being in and around nature will remind us of the God spirit in each one of us and reset our outlook. It will become a remembered way, not a new way, of our real purpose which is to keep that feeling with us always.

Menopause at Thirty-Nine?

While working as an independent contractor in Louisville, I was approached by one of our technicians in between patients. She expressed that she'd just had an emotional outbreak after talking to her mom, as well as a few recent incidents of night sweats, which were new to her. She related no history of cough or previous lung disease and no other signs of being unwell. She thought it was very strange that she was emotionally volatile, as she in fact prided herself on being emotionally steady, so this volatility for no reason was very out of character. Further, she'd never had PMS and didn't have her period because she had a Mirena intrauterine device (IUD) for birth control. She'd also tested negative for pregnancy.

She asked me if there might be a work up for her symptoms, which she thought were menopausal, and I told her that yes, there was a panel of hormones that could be tested to see if the ovaries had in fact begun to decrease production and go into hibernation, known as menopause. What a clever name: backward it means "pausing from men," which is in fact true. Menopause is akin to reverse puberty, when women take inventory of what they have learned from their relationships and integrate these lessons to move into the higher wisdom of maturity.

I then ordered a whole panel of menopause labs for the technician: FSH, LH, estrogen, and so on. In the meantime, I encouraged her to eat natural, good fats in her diet, as these were the body's source of all hormone production. Good fats come from plants and fish, such as fish oil, virgin olive oil, avocados, and flax seed. I stressed to her that she should buy them in a pure state, not in food that had been fried or processed at high temperatures, which leave the essential oils in the fat rancid. Most sincerely, the only thing the body can do with a fat that has been ruined under those conditions is to slap it on your backside as fat! If we include more unadulterated fats, we can give our own hormonal levels a boost. Plus, certain foods such as soybeans, found in the popular edamame beans, contain natural estrogens.

When I returned a week later, I invited the technician to come into a room to discuss her labs. She initially wanted to discuss them out in the hallway, but I insisted, based on the sensitive nature and the questions I would need to ask her. I began with the explanation that a panel of blood work is a snapshot of your body at one point in time and is not a true, whole representative of what is going on; athough, the panel can act as a guide. Her labs had come back negative for menopause, and all of her levels looked to be on track with a menstruating adult female. To this I added that I'd need to ask her a few more questions, as the symptoms she was having were real, even though they didn't show up in blood work.

"It can take years to develop the blood work of a fully menopausal woman," I told her. I then asked about her menstrual periods in adolescence, and she responded they had always been normal and that she had no history of early menopause in her family. I continued by asking about the medications she was on. She told me she took Celexa for depression and Synthroid for hypothyroidism.

Then I asked about her libido. At that point I felt her unease, her need to be up at the front desk, and her need to "keep it together," so I put a little show on to help draw her out with humor. As I sat beside her on the exam table, I said: "Have you always been *'vav.xvooooom*!" I shook my chest with my arms out. "Or have you always been more reserved, like this?" I said while I batted my eyelashes, crossed my legs, and looked shyly toward her.

She answered me by saying she'd felt ten feet tall and bulletproof during her twenties, which I took to mean she'd thought herself to be, "Vavavoom!" When I asked what had changed, she stated that at thirty years old, she'd married a man she didn't trust and was divorced ten years later. I understood her undertones and so expanded on the thought: "You suppressed your sexuality because that would be acquiescing to the enemy?" She agreed wholeheartedly.

Even though she'd been divorced for three years she was still in the same state, and though she'd been dating on and off, she hadn't yet returned to her premarriage state of joy.

When I asked why, she said, "I feel like I wasted ten years of my life." I mentioned that everything that happens to us does so to teach us a lesson, and if we see it in that way, it becomes a tool for our empowerment.

"There is something from that experience that you haven't let go of yet," I stated. "For if you had, you'd feel like a new person after the divorce."

I continued to explain that physically she was in a wonderful new life, but emotionally she was still reliving the relationship, and that had caused the way she'd been feeling. By having suppressed the feelings, she'd only succeeded in putting up a wall around herself, which had continued to become harder and harder to push down. This is why emotional outbursts surprise us; it's a pressure valve. If feelings are ignored too long, the valve can burst without warning.

To get at the heart of the matter, I then explained that stress perceived by the body, especially in the form of a repetitive negative thought, is a stressor because it carries a vibration that gets in the way of the body's wisdom for perfect health. Health of the body is the default; only when we interfere with our brooding natures does the body then become stressed by our mental/emotional influence. We need only look to two cells to demonstrate how the whole body is put together into a whole functional human without one thought from us!

"Health has *always* been about how we *feel,*" I explained. "If a person were to come in and just simply say, 'Find what is wrong with me,' I could do many tests and x-rays, and maybe find a heel spur. However, if I ask if the heel spur bothered the person and they said no, then have I really found what is wrong with them? Only half of heel spurs are symptomatic, even if they are in the same place, the same size, and so on.

"So that is why we are here," I continued, "because your feelings of menopausal symptoms are your body giving you the following message: 'We are headed this way with our current level of vitality; is this what you want?'

"If menopause at thirty-nine is no problem, then great, allow it," I explained, "but make sure that it's not a lack of vitality from feeling a waste of ten years, which is advancing the aging process and making you feel old before your time.

"You have a choice," I said emphatically. "Nurture your body, eat good fats, sort through the old relationship baggage that you've kept with you, and then let it go. If you still have menopausal symptoms, then fine. But don't be surprised if the new vitality you feel brings you back to a younger you, with increased libido, a new, rewarding relationship, and relief of the symptoms," I finished.

She hesitated, almost as if disappointed that the focused control she'd had of herself for so long hadn't been functioning, so much so that even her doctor saw it. Sometimes that alone is a good start.

Amy E. Coleman, MD

A Dry Cough for Five Weeks

The last patients of the day on a Saturday, a couple had waited for an hour to be seen. A fidgety woman in her mid-thirties sat on the exam room table with an older husband in a chair by her side. The atmosphere of the room had been charged when I'd walked in, coupled with the feeling of being in the middle of a shopping mall during the peak of the winter holiday shopping season. There was more to this than a little cough I thought to myself before any words had passed between us. I introduced myself and saw the woman bite the side of her lip, perhaps out of nervous habit. She squirmed and told me she didn't like doctors.

"I don't either. I don't ever see one unless I'm at work and accidentally look in the mirror," I said, laughing. "I don't wear a white coat if that helps. Look, we almost have the same shoes," I said, eager to get her mind off the situation. Our matching black loafers seemed like a good diversion.

She then began to tell me about a mild dry cough she'd been experiencing for the last month or so, which she thought had been irritated by cigarette smoke. At this there was an accusatory stab toward her husband, who sat quietly. The room bristled with her comment. I asked her the usual questions, looking for reasons for the occurrence of the cough. As a school athlete, she'd had a history of reactive airway conditions that caused her to need albuterol before major exertion. There was no history of hospitalized asthma or pneumonia, and she hadn't been on any medications; she was otherwise healthy and in no major distress. I was glad to rule out any infection by looking in her ears, nose, and throat. Her lungs were clear and didn't sound tight or wheezy.

I deduced that she had a mild exacerbation of a reactive airway. She'd need to use an albuterol inhaler and a stronger corticosteroid inhaler daily to prevent a flare-up. In the meantime, I explained that she'd need to remove any factors that worsened her breathing, such as excessive dust, pet dander, or whatever seemed to worsen it.

Her husband quickly chimed in and said, "That means all the dogs and cats, dear."

24

"Are you feeling tight in the chest?" I asked my patient. The dynamics of the room told me yes from the sheer tension I was feeling in my own chest from being in their company.

"Yes," she admitted. "My mother-in-law is living with us right now. It started around the time she moved in," she said, which made the correlation between the two.

"What do you do to help with being so stressed?" I asked.

"Have a drink!" she exclaimed.

At this, I warned that the initial relaxing effects of alcohol last for only an hour or two, to be replaced with a depressant effect for the next eighteen hours, leaving the person feeling less than able to handle stress in their lives. Over time and with repeated use, the depressant effect becomes intensified by anxiety after the initial relaxing effect. While I was sure to indicate that I felt there was any problem for this patient, it was still a good fact to be made aware of.

I continued to say that alcohol changes the architecture of sleep, decreasing the amount of deep sleep, or REM, intervals, so regular heavy drinkers sleep lighter with less of the truly restful sleep, waking less refreshed and more sleep deprived. My intention was to guide her to a better-stress coping strategy given that she seemed very sensitive and worn down due to having gone toe to toe with the matriarch of the family in the house.

"Look," I began, "you aren't going to change your mother-in-law. She has developed a strong sense of her opinion and will hold to those beliefs until she passes on. It probably has served her family well at some point, helping to glue the family together and moving mountains when needed. You don't look at your dogs in the backyard when they're barking at something over the fence, and exclaim exhaustedly, at your wit's end, 'Why don't you stop barking? It's killing me!'" I said in an exaggerated, dramatic effect, as if I were a worn-out woman on her last leg.

"Instead," I went on, "you understand that your dogs are feeling a little insecure about something past the hedges, and it spurs them into a sense to defend their insecurity by barking. Your mother-in-law is the same way. She feels a bit insecure and wants to defend her position by barking. And that's all she is doing—barking!"

They looked at each other at that point, and then the husband said, "How do you know my mother so well?"

Without pausing, I stated to the patient that she'd be better off addressing her mother-in-law when her own energy and well-being were intact, such as after a workout or a walk with the dogs. The reason she continued to feel unwell was because she wasn't remaining true to who she was. She allowed her mother-in-law to conform her to the negative thoughts that didn't fit her, and the patient, unhappy about having felt so uncomfortable, had become addled and frazzled, magnifying usual mild irritations to major frustrations. Her husband, stressed about having seen the world war in his home continue, had begun smoking more and more heavily, which just frustrated his wife even more.

The patient agreed that she would take better care of herself, having understood that she could only help someone by presenting her best self, which meant giving her the permission to spend quality time maintaining her own peace of mind through the endeavor that felt best for her. This change in perception would help with irritation in every form, from relationships to inflamed airways.

There was a sigh of relief, and I then felt relaxed in that room, as did they. I offered a steroid injection to obliterate any remnant of bronchial inflammation so they'd be on their way with no perceivable, bothersome symptoms. This would last her until she picked up her inhalers, if she still needed them.

They then asked if I would be their doctor. I said was glad to. I gave them my business card and told them to keep in touch as I had plans for a clinic to open near where I lived. I explained that it would probably be too far away, as they were one hour north. They disagreed and told me they'd make the drive without hesitation. After hugs all around, they were discharged. As they left, I felt that the difference in treating the whole person versus treating only a symptom truly made the study of health a worthy experience.

CHAPTER 3

Blessings in Camouflage

Conversation with a Colleague

After having made coffee in the break room, my colleague sat down at the table behind me. I turned around and noticed that since I'd last seen him, he'd lost more weight. He already had the build of a marathon runner by default, and so the weight loss had become very noticeable; his cheeks and eyes had looked more sunken, and he'd not been clean-shaven. Over the past six months he'd been grappling with the promotion from physician to clinic director, and the strain had obviously been taking its toll. Since I worked at the clinic on a contract basis once or twice a week, I'd been able to see the changes very acutely. After a deliberate pause and deep breath, he began telling me how it all had been going for him lately, hands folded in prayer under his nose.

My colleague had a military background and was a devoted medical unit commander for the army who had taken great care of his brigade. He'd always been willing to step up to perform the next hardest task, but here, under the command of the insurance conglomerate that owned the clinic, he'd found that there was no end to the stepping up part. He'd been handed a new mandate to see post-injury patients for follow-ups every three to five days instead of every seven, which greatly increased the daily flow of patients through the clinic. As a result, he'd been working to improve the process and had offered to brainstorm potential solutions with me. This was something we'd always loved to do together.

The former soldier in him had often brought out the soldier in me, since I was a former air force officer. We'd mastermind plans for the clinic as if they were war games and calculate battle moves. He felt comfortable relating to the clinic as the battleground, and I went right along. The front desk administrative clerks were the infantry, and when something went wrong, it was of course deemed a "charlie foxtrot." E-mails back and forth between us were signed "Wilco" and "Roger that," and we kept our officer titles out of respect for each other.

He'd been wrapping his head around the concept of this new surge in patient flow and so asked me for any ideas. I suggested that he could make rounds in the physical therapy department that was attached to our clinic, where many of our injured workers were stretching, massaging, pushing, and pulling their way to getting better three times per week. This method of follow-up would allowed us to lay hands on the patients at the newly mandated frequency yet would still allowed us flexibility as the providers. Unfortunately, after further thought we realized that the patient wouldn't be able to be charged for an office visit, which was much more profitable and a main reason for the demand to increase follow-ups. My colleague, as big-hearted as he was, was still determined to find a way to stay within the new proposed regulations.

At this, and after having seen his physical condition, I'd begun to rant. "You know, even Einstein said that no problem can be fixed from the level that it was created. There needs to be a more aerial, visionary view of the problem; to get out of the weeds, so to speak." I realized then that he'd been in a reactive state to problems in the clinic, with a knee-jerk reaction from the stress he'd been feeling.

"With your mind-set, you'll never have enough toes or fingers to block all the places in the dam that are leaking," I told him. "A reactionary mode is when one acts out of a place of sheer panic and is never the right mind-set to find the true solution." I likened this to my horse who, on a good day, upon passing a gum wrapper on the ground, sees it as what it is, glances in the direction of it, and pays it no mind. On the contrary, when my horse is sensing threat or fear, a simple gum wrapper on the ground becomes an alien and sends my horse running at top speed away from this invader with heart pounding and adrenaline pumping.

Both are solutions to the same problem, but both are made at completely different states of mind. This seemed to make good sense to him, and he nodded in agreement. He repeated, "Gum wrapper alien" out loud, as if he liked the ring of it.

He duly noted that, when approached from a place of true helpfulness, things he found interesting would mean he was able to diligently work without fatigue all day long. He admitted that some of the things he'd been asked to do lately drained his energy, and he'd seen no need or justification for the tasks. He then stated that he could've started dropping more of his workouts in order to get the tasks over with and then extended other ideas that, as I watched, just drained him more and more as he talked through them.

I spoke up at that point. "You need to listen to how the perceived solution to the problem makes you feel," I said. "If the solution you have in mind makes you feel depleted, then it is not the right solution!"

He agreed and seemed to see that he'd been stuck in a wheel for a little while, unaware of having been overextended, despite the fact that it was written all over his face. He then went back and buried himself in his paperwork, and I went to cover seeing his patients that day. We both knew we'd be there for each other, and that made a big difference.

A few days later I was working a quiet weekend shift at the clinic and spotted a newly taped reminder at the base of his computer monitor. It was a workspace we both shared. Among a sea of sticky notes that formed his to-do list sat the taped message, which read as follows:

> May today there be peace within.
> May you trust God that you are
> Exactly where you are meant to be.
> May you not forget the infinite
> Possibilities that are born of faith.
> May you use those gifts that you have received,
> And pass on the love that has been given to you.
> May you be content knowing you are a child of God.
> Let this presence settle into your bones,
> And allow your soul the freedom to sing, dance, praise,
> and love.
>
> —St. Therese of Lisieux

Seeking Approval

My patient, bearing a resemblance to Jimmy Buffet without the Hawaiian shirt, sat smiling on the exam table. A lean man in his late fifties, he'd hurt his back on the job a few weeks before and had come in today with the results of his MRI. He was already aware of the results: degenerative joints along his vertebrae as well as a mild bulging disc. There were also signs of osteophytes between the vertebrae. All in all, it was a normal image of an aging back still doing some pretty heavy lifting.

The spine, with its alignment of vertebra-disc-vertebra-disc, is a great shock absorber. The "pillows" or disks between each vertebrate become less fluffy with age, just as a chair cushion that is sat on for years and years becomes flat. This brings the vertebrae closer in vicinity to one another, creating an area of higher friction. The ends of the vertebrae can sense this and so begin to create more bone in an effort to pad the area, much as a callous forms on the bottom of your foot from excessive rubbing and load-bearing.

Unfortunately, as well meaning as this callousing process of the bone is, the creation of jagged points of bone called osteophytes, are the result. They then can impale and stab the local surrounding tissue when involved in extensive activity that causes flare-ups of muscular back pain and discomfort.

This gentleman had been working in the asphalt paving industry for years. He'd worked his way up from the most menial job all the way to supervisor and had worked happily for many years until layoffs and the shifting economy found him having to accept a job again as a basic laborer. His first thought had been how he could have come so far, just to be right back where he started. Without sounding judgmental, he mentioned that no one on the job had cared to help out unless they had to, so he often had been the one who'd stepped up to the plate and had gotten "in the trenches." He'd moved pipes and heavy equipment while younger, more physically capable men had simply sat back and watched. He wasn't at all angry, though it was clear that he didn't agree with the behavior of his colleagues. He prided himself on doing the right thing.

Most of the population has a bulging disc, though if they do any significant lifting or apply frequent pressure to their backs over time, very few require any intervention. A bulging disc is a sign to let up on the intensity of strain on the back and allow correction to take place. So I discussed with him the idea that due to the wear and tear on his back, heavy laboring may be best left to those with stronger backs. He agreed, especially since he'd been looking to be rehired at the supervisory levels again. The one issue with that idea had been that his wife, a generally negative person, had been telling him over and over that he was too old to be hired for the management positions.

"Great!" I said. "Let her be exactly as she is, and thank her for it, as you do not need anyone's approval to do the next thing you know you need to do for yourself anyway.

"As a matter of fact," I continued, "the contrast of your differing opinions works as a trampoline to give you extra momentum when you disagree with her. Like yin and yang, extreme opposites allow us to see what we don't want and/or disagree with so that we know strongly which direction to start walking toward what we do want. A strong negative influence is often more powerful than a weakly positive influence, like a magnet, so is meant to work more powerfully for you."

"When you both get up in heaven and are looking back one day," I joked, "she'll probably tell you that she was negative not only to dissuade you from your mission but to also give you the self-directed ability and discomfort from within your own self to do the right thing. This way you act out of your own self and not because you have the approval of anyone around you to begin it. That intention is much more powerful than requiring approval of others to begin."

He looked at me and smiled, shaking his head. "You are amazing," he said. "You come in here like an angel and tell me just what I needed to hear."

"It's really just a simple truth for all of us to remember," I explained. He mentioned that he'd gotten away from his faith for many years, but just a few days ago he'd found himself back at his church and had been taken aside by a pastor he'd known before. He'd also encouraged him to step out boldly in the direction of what he wanted.

He then told me about the wonderful feeling of being back in the arms of faith and peace in that church and smiled when he remembered the words of his grandchild who had sat by his side that day and said, "Can we come here a lot? I like it here." That day of having received support in church, combined with my words of support, meant he knew what he needed to do. I told him that it was common to receive help when you needed it. This was especially true when you were on track with what you wanted and were open to guidance.

After having examined the patient, I asked if I might pray for him, and he was very happy to oblige. I held his hand and prayed that he'd be able to follow his own voice within, focusing only on his own and the guidance he'd receive.

I had faith that there was a great plan for him and a place to share all his gifts of self-motivation, inspiration, and experience from which others could benefit. I prayed that he'd take his eyes away from the door that was closing to instead look behind him and see the one that was opening for him. I prayed for him to have the courage to step boldly and assuredly toward constructing a better-suited working environment. I prayed that he would have the faith during the transition to know that he was not in limbo but a state of supported, divinely directed free fall into a better opportunity and to trust in the faith of God's plan, and allow, without friction, the change to happen. At the close of prayer, I thanked him for the opportunity to see the lesson unfold in his life. With this, we were reminded of the importance that perception starts from within and not from any other person, event, or external circumstance.

As he checked out, I heard him speak warmly about his encounter to the technician. Her monotone response of, "Really?" demonstrated that she hadn't understood how a simple visit regarding back pain could've left him feeling so refreshed.

A Prickly Encounter

My nurse presented a short introduction of the patient I was about to see: "She's anemic and just started an iron supplement. She also hasn't been taking her seizure medicine anymore because it makes her feel bad. She wants to know if we can test the levels of the medicine to see if it is helping her or not."

"Well, there won't be any levels detected if she hasn't been taking the medication," I said.

I then entered the room and introduced myself, and before me sat a forty-year-old woman who'd had a "buzzy" demeanor. Not busy, but *buzzy*. Being in her presence was akin to standing very close to a main power station. There was intensity to her gaze, and she spoke with crisp, well-defined speech and knew what she wanted.

She was unaware that her right foot flexed at the ankle spontaneously and sharply to the right quickly when she spoke about matters that created some static within her, much like a warning, "I might bite" sign. It reminded me of a rattlesnake that also telegraphs his intentions with the rattling device on the end of its tail. I didn't think she knew that she did this.

"How long have you worked here? Are you new?" she asked.

"No," I answered calmly. "I've worked here for a year and a half."

As we continued to converse, she spoke about being diagnosed with iron-deficiency anemia by her OB-GYN months ago, but she hadn't been taking anything for it until the last few days when she'd found some pills in the back of the cabinet, an iron supplement from a previous treatment, though they'd hurt her stomach after only a few days.

I then mentioned that the absorption of iron was difficult at best, made worse by the fact that this heavy metal was concentrated into a pill form that can sit heavy in the stomach. This was especially true if the person had difficulty with digestion, such as diabetes or irritable bowel syndrome. These conditions further slow the already slow breakdown process of the supplements. I also mentioned that there were other more natural, easier-to-absorb options, so I'd recommended she try Floridix, a suspension of plant-derived iron sources.

"You know it is recommended that you eat your spinach for iron?" I continued. "Well, this is the squeezed collection of the juices of those plants with the highest levels of iron, in a suspension form, not a pill."

I said that the price of thirty dollars may seem high, but one bottle would last a good month at least so the investment would be a good one. I also told her that she'd get more elemental iron by eating out of a cast iron pan. Pure elemental iron rubs off from this surface with each use, evidenced by the fact that if the pan gets wet, it'll be rusted by the next morning.

She then asked about helping the absorption of iron with B12. I related that there are conditions that prevent a person from absorbing iron due to a deficiency in the ability to assimilate B12.

"There are tests done for that, which are not done here, that would diagnose this problem known as pernicious anemia," I answered. "However, the simplest thing would just be to supplement B12 every day. It's a water-soluble vitamin that flushes out in your urine every day. You can never overdose. The best way for this to be absorbed is sublingually. It is best bought in a dropper bottle with three to four drops placed under the tongue with the mouth kept closed for thirty seconds."

At this point, the patient began to get around to what was really on her mind. She wanted to know about her medication for seizures, known as Lamictal. She was concerned that it might affect her kidneys or liver. In fact, she mentioned that her BUN, or blood urea nitrogen level, which tests for kidney function, had been mildly elevated according to her last test results. She spoke with a sharp edge, stressing that she would go to another doctor to test these levels if it was necessary.

"That blood result could have been explained by being a touch under-hydrated," I stated.

She admitted that she didn't drink enough water. She went on to mention again that she wondered whether her liver had been damaged, and at that statement her foot flexed upward quickly in a darting manner.

"First," I said, "Lamictal does metabolize in the liver, but if you haven't been taking it for a month, there would likely be no elevation in levels because the liver is no longer working overtime to break it down. This is what drives enzymes up.

"If you drank alcohol, had a handful of Tylenol, and took cholesterol medications," I explained, "your liver enzyme levels would be elevated because the liver would be producing much more enzyme to process all of the medications' components. The feelings of a hangover remind you what elevated liver functions feel like: fatigue, difficulty concentrating, and nausea are the most common symptoms. If they are extremely elevated, then jaundice arises."

However, she didn't have any of these symptoms.

"Why were you treated with an antiseizure medication?" I asked.

"Because I had seizures!" she hissed back.

At this defensive response, I had to laugh a bit and feigned a little frustrated scream with my fists closed, looking up at heaven for a moment in plea.

I answered slowly, "I know you had seizures, so let's back up. Did you have a small shake on one side of your body, or did it occur throughout your body?"

She told me that she'd had several grand mal seizures.

"Did you have a sleep-deprived EEG?" I asked, in order to gain a better understanding into what was tested to consider the type of seizures.

"Yes," she stated. "And I had a grand mal seizure while being tested."

"Did you have a concussion, or fall and hit your head, or lose consciousness before your seizures began?" I felt that in this questioning it was as though I was tiptoeing through a minefield.

"Well, my father slammed my head against a wall repeatedly as a child when he was angry with me," she responded matter of factly.

"Oh, I see, and you have been on the Lamictal since then?" I asked gently, keeping the tone professional yet empathetic.

"I've been on it for ten years," she said, "and I have worked in highly professional jobs and have done quite well, despite them making me sleepy and feeling out of it. But lately, I've been cutting back and even not taking them, and I have been seizure-free for ten years. I like the way I feel without them. I have so much more energy and vibrancy."

I then saw that this was a very empowered woman who'd simply been looking to receive some positive medical support for her decision to stop the medication.

"I know that I feel much better when I get plenty of rest and eat right," she said simply. Her idea was valiant: seizure-free through healthy living. However, it wasn't the source of the issue.

At this, I gave a bit of background on medications.

"There are people that take a pill every day and believe greatly in the effects it'll have on their health. As a matter of fact, even if it were a sugar pill, it would indeed alter the body for the good. The mind is *that* strong. I would never discontinue a pill that a person felt this way about, unless medically necessary," I said.

"However, if the person takes a pill and there is a great resistance within them to take it, then that's a whole other battle of the will," I continued. "For example, the doctor says to take it, but you feel that it doesn't help you, so you don't believe in the therapy. You live in your body every day and know how it feels, and want to listen to its wisdom, but you are told to 'just take the pill.' In this instance, a pill will have more negative effects than positive. You might perhaps feel more side effects from it.

"Unfortunately," I went on, "society has created a current medical model where doctors work within a risk management model of medicine. It is a litigious field; doctors are conservative in making their recommendations because of fear of a bad outcome. If they'd told you to stop taking the medication, for example, and you'd had a grand mal seizure, then they might've lost their license if you'd sued them. To understand more about why you had a health problem that needed medication, you must realize the power that your mind and body have in your response to negative events."

I then told her the story of when I was in Iraq among war-torn victims and survivors who'd suffered grand mal seizures despite no previous history of seizures.

"There is a great discord when a shocking event occurs," I said. "The amount of resistance in trying to process something that seems beyond all ability to understand can throw the mind into a short circuit. Trying to understand how someone such as your father, who is supposed to love and nurture you, can treat you in such disregard, all the while healing from the physical trauma of the abuse is enough to send the mind into a frenzy. Seizures can result from this competing resistance. However, anything that happens to you is truly there to mine the lesson, not the suffering."

"I dare you," I said with an intense glare, "to go and research the top three people for which you've always felt a deep sense of admiration and respect. You will assuredly find that, in their younger years, they experienced a very dark time of turbulence and what could've be seen as a hard lot in life. The level of what could be perceived as pain and suffering may even pull at your heartstrings. However, they "got" it—the wisdom of seeing events in their life from a bird's-eye view. They understood that it was never meant to tear them apart but rather to catapult them farther along toward self-reliance and strength by calling upon their own will and determination for something better."

I felt that this wonderful woman had put so much of the past behind her and had then stepped out on her own power to create the life she wanted for herself. Finally in a better place, she was ready to seek a more peaceful life for herself, though to do so she'd first had to give herself validation for being off the medication, and to forgive the past and her own forward-charging, take-no-prisoners demeanor. I mentioned to her that there had been a time in my own life for bulldozing and charging full steam ahead, but there was no longer any need for that. I'm in the clear and have adopted more peaceful measures.

"When you're running out of the forest with the army chasing you, you don't want a white swan to float you out. You want a galloping horse to get you to safety. So own and thank the part of you that was strong enough to carry you to safety. Don't judge it. Once you own it and thank it, then you can properly retire it for a better fit for you at this time in your life," I explained.

"At forty years old with children and all the wisdom you have gathered, you can now develop finesse and learn that gain does not come with only pain. And you are well on your way. For example, today you went from this," I said, staring ahead with a steely glare and vibrating, as if I was experiencing a permanent chill running up my spine, and making a vibrating noise like a power grid transformer, "to this." Here I took a deep breath and showed the softness of expression and relaxed demeanor that was a reflection of her at that moment.

"You see yourself as being ready for a transformation, and it's happening," I told her. "The you that you want to be is just beneath the surface, left only with the thin film of the old resistant, hard-driving self. The reason it bothers you so much is because it's similar to the last five pounds to lose on a diet. You'll notice it more when there's just a small amount left to remove.

"So you see, listening to the wisdom of your body to be seizure free for life is about more than just getting enough sleep and eating right. It's once and for all patching and healing the old scars and thanking but leaving behind for good the parts that do not serve you anymore," I said.

"But it's not just up to you to align. You must understand that we are all spirit, mind, and body equally, and understanding how to get in touch with that spirit part of you that anchors and keeps you grounded is paramount. Whether it's your Jesus, Buddha, highest self, and so on, you don't need to have a church or a priest—simply the quiet intention of wanting to know that part of yourself, in a quiet state. Meditation and prayer is a way toward this, a way to quiet your mind, and move out of your own way," I finished, in a soothing, mellow tone, with rhythmic breaths, feeling myself further slip into stillness and relaxation. I felt her quietness intensify in response, and I brought it to her attention.

"You're in a quiet, centered state now; how do you like it?" I asked.

"Very much," she said. "I want to live like this."

"So," I went on, "we started simply on the surface with iron deficiency and a need for checking labs, to one layer down, which was the feeling of wanting to finally get off of seizure medications. Then, we went further down the rabbit hole about the power of your mind; then even deeper to the role that forgiveness and the spirit play. We've covered a lot in one visit!"

At this she said, "Several things you've said have really resonated with me today. I do want to learn meditation. This visit is just a series of events that have happened to me this week that are all just pointing in the same direction."

"That's how the universe works," I stated. "When you put out your intention and beliefs, little evidences of these thoughts come to us, as if God is saying, 'Is this what you want?' We're like magnets—we attract what are a match to ourselves."

"Even my brother said I was on the right track recently," she continued. "I can't wait to tell him about our visit today."

"Don't be surprised if it is hard to find words that really capture the feeling of it," I cautioned her.

"We made an excellent hire in you," she stated, spoken as the true human resources executive she was.

"Oh, me? I'm just an independent contractor, filling in for the medical director ever since he left," I said with a smile and a good-bye, and she smiled warmly back.

At the Edge of a Stroke

"This one may need to go to the ER; his blood pressure is 210/105," my medical assistant told me, referring to the next patient who was there for a commercial driver's physical.

This was high enough to be considered a crisis level for stroke or heart attack, if the patient had symptoms such as headache, nausea, or chest pain.

"He might live there," I replied.

"Living there" is a term used when a patient has had high blood pressure so long that his or her body adjusts to the elevation and no longer feels any headache or symptoms from it. It's still a health risk for stroke and heart disease, but the patient feels fine, and lowering the blood pressure to normal (130/80 or lower) without treading very slowly could make him or her very sick.

"Does he have any symptoms?" I asked.

"None," was the answer.

As I stepped into the room, I saw a small-built man dressed in a neon green shirt and jeans. He had a large Celtic cross on his forearm and as I would determine later, the face of Jesus tattooed on his right chest. The patient had looked pitiful and full of chronic worry, with lines etched deep into his face.

I had his previous paperwork from his physical a year earlier that showed his blood pressure had been normal at that time. When I compared this with the high blood pressure my medical assistant had recorded and asked what had happened to cause such a discrepancy, the patient described to me the details of how he'd lost his house, gone through a divorce, and used his entire life's savings to pay these expenses.

He then explained that he'd always worked because he wanted to, not because he needed to, due to his $50,000 in savings. He'd always considered it as his safety net so that he'd never have to live paycheck to paycheck; however, since it was gone, he felt as though he'd lost everything.

"It's just hard," he stated, exhausted. His face was contorted like someone with the wind blowing at gale strength, head-on, or as if squinting against the sun. "Plus if I don't pass my physical, I can't do my job."

"Yes," I stated, "but this way of thinking drives up your blood pressure. We are very appreciative of the job you do and are always willing to work with you to help you keep doing your job. When someone feels threatened, as you do, his or her body reacts like a threatened animal would, and as a result the heart races and the pulse pounds.

"Sometimes," I went on, "we can get so worried about something that we create an even bigger problem than the one we think we have. When you're in a worried state of mind, I could put you in the middle of Hawaii on a beautiful beach and you'd still not be able to enjoy it. Something would creep up that felt missing or wrong. Or if you won the lottery you'd be scared about the security of the money you'd won. In the worried state of mind there are only three real thoughts: what has threatened me, what will threaten me, and what is threatening me."

I then pointed at the eight-inch tattoo of the Celtic cross on his right forearm and asked, "Do you use faith in this to help you?"

"Yes," he answered, "I used to, but it's hard to keep faith."

"Well, it's harder the way you're doing it," I said. "You're trying to manage your daily job, organize your vision for the future, and control all the elements of nature and others around you. You are not God!" I stated. "You've got it turned upside down. It's not meant for you to take on such large matters but to leave that in trust into His hands, with the knowledge that He is love and will provide what you need. You're meant to be the daily manager of your life, not the CEO. You don't have the visionary tools for the job of God."

"Yeah, but it is hard," he said again.

"It's all about perspective," I continued. "Have you ever worked for a great boss? A great CEO makes your job easy."

The patient added, "And you make it easy for him too."

"That's right," I went on, "because you're working together. You think that fifty thousand dollars was pure security, but if you'd had a major health experience, such as a heart attack and stroke that required a bypass surgery plus sixteen weeks of stroke rehabilitation, with six weeks of cardiac rehab, your fifty thousand dollars wouldn't have even covered your needs. You'd then be reminded the hard way that the fifty thousand dollars had never been the security net you thought it was.

"God really wants to help you," I explained, "but he can't if you can't get your eyes off of that fifty thousand dollars. He wants to give you much more than that, but you have to trust and create a space for him to help you. This is why God was so adamant about not having idols. Everything comes and goes in your life: people, jobs, relationships, pets; all external things to teach us each day that nothing stays except what is eternal, and that is the spirit. I'm here today to help teach you this in a less painful and traumatic way than where you were headed toward."

At this, he rubbed his arms and mentioned that he had goose bumps.

"What do you think those mean?" I asked.

He looked at me, puzzled.

"It means that whatever is going on in the moment you have that feeling is the direction you need to pay attention to because it's guidance in the right direction," I stated firmly.

"The further away you drift from this feeling of warmth, love, and wellness, the more and more horrible, tense, and out of control you'll feel because you move farther and farther away from what God means for you to have. You're trying so hard to keep such tight control of everything that God isn't able to help you because you insist on seeing things your way. And you know the touching part? He loves you so much that he'll even allow you to do what you want, how you want it, rather than interfere. But I can tell you right now that it was no mistake that you came here today.

He couldn't get through to you by normal channels, and so I'm here to give you the message since I'm physically right in front of you. I work for him every day," I said.

"I prayed that I would get help today, in the car before I came in here," he said.

"There are no mistakes and no coincidences," I stated.

"It's hard," he repeated for the third time. He touched his chest and said, "I know all this, and I have him right here." He then showed me his right chest, with the portrait of Jesus' face.

"Well, now walk the walk," I said encouragingly. "I also went through a time of divorce, move, and shifting jobs, all at the same time. I didn't know which direction was up, and I didn't trust myself to put any parts of my life back together. I literally prayed with every step: 'Dear Lord, I don't trust myself at all. I don't trust myself to do the simplest thing I thought I could handle. I don't trust my judgment because it is shortsighted. I don't trust my actions because I'm fearful. At this time I need your guidance, and I surrender to it.'

"And if every day, you start with that prayer, say it through the day and at night, I guarantee you will see the changes that come in a miraculous way," I said.

"Can I just take you with me everywhere I go? Things would be so different if I could," he asked.

"You don't need me," I replied.

"You would make a great evangelist," he added.

"I don't even go to church," I said, laughing. "You don't need a preacher or a place of worship, because it's within you wherever you go."

I then asked him to begin to think of five things he was appreciative of in his life.

"I'm appreciative of you!" he answered.

"And I'm appreciative of you," I replied. "For every time I teach this, I share the feelings you have—I felt the goose bumps you had, and I'm thankful to you for coming in so that we could share it together. Now, why don't we pray? It is the best medicine we have."

I then sat beside him on the exam table and held his right hand in both of my hands. I asked that he be open to receive guidance and to be able to understand that he was never meant to take on so much but to trust in love and faith for God to create for him on his behalf just what he needed for his life. I prayed that he would be able to look beyond his setbacks for the blessings that lay in store for him.

Once I finished, he described feeling warm, calm, and happy. "I want to feel this good all the time," he said.

"You can, if you do what I suggest," I answered.

I then fastened the blood pressure cuff slowly on his right upper arm, pumping the cuff up. Letting the pressure go, I listened.

"Your blood pressure went from 210/110 to 148/95, and it was all a matter of changing your perspective," I said. "Nothing physically changed in your life, but your mind and heart decided on a different state. Because of that, I can now offer you a three-month temporary card to continue driving," I told him.

"You'll need to see your doctor tomorrow and make sure your blood pressure and blood sugar stay controlled. He may put you on a blood pressure medicine to bring it down a little further. And with what you learned, you will actually be able to be in the right mind-set to take care of yourself, and to remember to take your medications," I finished.

"I can't thank you enough," he said. "Can I come back and see you?"

"Sure, I work here on Wednesdays, and you can call ahead and make sure I'm here. My name is Dr. Coleman."

"I can remember that," he said. "My best friend's name is Coleman."

Chronic Pain

An employee who works the front desk at the clinic came to see me, with her hands clenched together nervously.

"My husband's neurologist thinks that he is having absence seizures and did an EEG. It didn't show anything, but the neurologist still started him on seizure medicine. Since then, my husband hasn't been doing well on it."

Absence is a type of seizure where one stares with emptiness into space for a time and is hard to rouse out of it. Her husband had had multiple neck fusion surgeries and was on antidepressant medications. He'd also been on high-dose narcotic medication for many years.

"Was it a sleep-deprived EEG?" I asked.

"No. It was a regular EEG, but there were fire alarms going off during the test! We asked the neurologist to repeat it, but he said that we didn't need to," she said in exasperation.

"Hmm," I said, frowning, "the quality of test can make a lot of difference, especially when it results in having to take a medication for the rest of your life."

I then told her a story about importance of the quality of testing. When I was in the military, I used to take care of the Special Forces teams, and they had quite a grueling indoctrination program of training. After six weeks, halfway through indoctrination training, they were required to take multiple tests for blood and a thorough physical in order to continue.

One trainee, who was first in his class at that stage, had a very soft heart murmur that showed up during the exam.

Murmurs are usually benign, or harmless, but can indicate a problem with the architecture of the heart. In this man's case, a chest echocardiogram was performed to see the real time images of the heart; they revealed that he had a bicuspid aortic valve. This is a rare valve variation with two segments instead of three. The two-segment variety forms a less than ideal flow cover for the aorta and increases the risk of aneurysm. If present, it's a disqualifying condition for the military Special Forces. When the trainee's commandant called me about this, they asked if there was anything left that could be done. It seemed such a waste of a good candidate to disqualify him when he was doing so well. I knew that echocardiograms were moving images whose results varied up to 30 percent depending on the experience level of the cardiologist reading the image. Plus, given that the echocardiogram had been done at Wilford Hall, a teaching hospital, meant that typically it was cardiologists in training that read the films, with the more experienced cardiologists only providing a verified signature, who were often in a hurry due to overseeing so many residents. I also knew this trainee's echocardiogram was imaged from the top of the heart, on the surface of the sternum; this view made it difficult to truly see the northernmost portion that contained the aorta and aortic valve.

I suggested a transesophageal echocardiogram, which requires sedation since the transducer must be placed into the esophagus, located just over the top of the aortic area. This offers a perfect view of the valve. To everyone's relief, this test showed a normal tricuspid aortic valve, and so the trainee was allowed to continue. The quality of a test can count for everything!

I then mentioned that she might want to seek a second opinion from a neurologist who would consider her concerns. She agreed and related that there had been a recommendation from a different neurologist that her husband could wear a monitor that would show any change in his brainwave as he became fatigued, usually at the end of the day, when the absence seizures were more likely to happen. Then, if there was indication of brain wave frequency problems, they would start him on a different trial medication. However, her husband had refused. He hadn't wanted any part of the medicine or that test.

I cautioned that it's not a good idea to take a pill when there is a lot of resistance. Pills alter body chemistry, but the patient's feelings that the pills will work also play a role: the placebo effect. On the other hand, when the patient despises taking their pills, then more of the side effects are felt, or the patient feels that the pills don't work at all. This negativity is called a nocebo effect and is well documented in medical literature.

"So he needs to tell himself it will help!" she said.

"Even that won't help if he doesn't truly believe it. It's like biting into celery with a fake smile and claiming that it's your favorite food," I explained. "No one believes you, and you definitely do not believe yourself. But if you cut a piece of the celery up and add peanut butter and raisins, and then really do think it is tasty, then that is authentic and believable. He takes other medications, doesn't he?"

"Yes, he takes narcotic pain medications, but they don't seem to help," she replied.

"They never will for chronic daily pain," I said, shaking my head. "They work well for acute pain that is a result of a recent surgery or procedure. They go right to the place to stop the pain; however, chronic pain is a whole different animal."

A negative feedback loop influences the effect of the medication when a person experiences pain over a long period of time. Also well documented is the way the brain and body are wired to perceive pain—it's almost as if a relationship forms with the pain. Instead of trying to feel better, chronic pain patients begin looking for the level of their pain before they even open their eyes in the morning. They learn to develop an intense, laser-like focus on it, like a sharpshooter or a military sniper. As a result, the nerve connections to this pain circuit are intensified and built up like a muscle that is always being flexed. At times, pain can be all a patient in chronic pain sees, just as a bodybuilder looking in the mirror may only study his or her figure. This constant interaction further develops the sensitivity of the pathways to feel the pain.

"Yes, and sometimes it's all he lives for. He'll go to work, come home, and go to sleep. He doesn't even want to try to do anything else," she explained sadly.

I mentioned that pain is complex. Then I recommended three books by Dr. Sarno: *The Divided Mind*, *Healing Back Pain*, and *The Mind Body Connection*. She thanked me and said she would read them. It was a brief interaction, but I prayed that she and her husband would find some help, as she greatly missed having her partner engaged in living his best life.

Close to the Breaking Point

My medical assistant told me that my next patient had recently been discharged from the Ridge, a psychiatric facility. As a condition, the man had promised his psychiatrist that he'd go and talk to someone before he "got that bad again."

"He's very angry and feels like his mind is racing out of control this morning," my assistant reported to me.

I asked her to buy me thirty minutes, which meant she'd block off some time before my next patient so I could have time for a quality visit. The clinic had been busy that week; seeing patients every five to fifteen minutes was commonplace.

When I walked into the room, I saw a man sitting slumped over in dramatic form on the exam table. His eyes looked up at me, but his head didn't move, which made him look even more menacing and angry. Despite this, I felt he had a mismatch in energy; this patient wasn't angry, he was frustrated, and so I immediately decided that he posed no threat to himself or to me.

He began to tell me that, for some unknown reason, he'd woken up feeling all out of sorts and mad with the world. It had been no better when he'd gotten to work: the smallest things had made him want to "throttle his coworker."

"I just wanted to be left alone," he said. "But he kept trying to help me, and I thought I was going to lose it or punch his lights out."

This patient obviously felt as if he was coming unglued, and it was unsettling to him. He went on to say that he was happily married, but his ex-wife continued to take him to court over issues he'd found ludicrous, such as allegations of having mistreated their daughter. His ex-wife was unhappy, and so she wanted to make sure he was unhappy too.

As I listened to his story, I couldn't help but feel something in common with the man. At certain times, I too had felt that anything might've set me off; a normal, daily interaction could've been a source of undue agitation.

"What you are feeling is a common human emotion," I said. "Sometimes, if we go to bed worried or angry about something, it stays with us all night long, and we wake up in the same emotion we felt when we went to bed. We may dream about it, or sleep tensely with our fists closed, as if we are ready to fight. This is not the best way to rest, which is why it is so important to resolve your anger before bed. Saying a prayer or meditation of appreciation, and moving your thoughts to those of love and thanksgiving, allows you to slip off into a dream state more restfully and peacefully. When you don't unplug from your anger before bed, you toil and toss in it all night and so are truly marinating in it for hours, which naturally continues when you wake."

I explained further that we as humans can experience a broad spectrum of emotions. We can identify with our basest, most primitive selves, acting and feeling threatened like an animal in a cage and therefore wanting to simply attack. Or we can get above the immediate situation and see it from a higher level, making it less personal and taking into account all sides of the story. When we do that, we make decisions and react in more diplomatic, thoughtful way.

Within the same one person, at any one time, is the ability to act out. The difference is that, when we feel as if what happens to us is deeply personalized, as if it is a direct attack on us as an individual, we have made the decision to choose the lowest energy form of response.

"We feel hurt and therefore have only hurt to give back. This is why you felt so uncomfortable this morning. I'm actually quite proud of you," I admitted. "Most people go throughout their whole day, enraged and seething, but place a superficial smile with which to greet the world as an outer coating. You, as genuine and transparent as you are, realize that you are better than that and so want to fix it instead of grinning and bearing it, and I applaud you for that. You know there is a part of you that can deal with this problem in a healthier, better-feeling way, and you will stand for no less than that."

I then asked if I could pray with him, and he didn't budge. I reached for his hand, yet he remained unmoved, so I prayed in place, not forcing the issue. After a prayer, I looked him over. He was still sitting on the exam room table in the same threatening way, but I felt that he'd softened.

I then asked if I could help with his posture and began to push his shoulders back. I placed my hand on his lower back, pressing in, while I pressed back at one shoulder with my other hand. I then placed his hands on his legs in a relaxed manner, taking them off of the sides of the exam room table where he'd held with a vice grip to either side. He still felt the need to play the part of what everyone had told him he was, but I'd seen a much better side of him. I continued to rearrange him, lifting his chin and pushing his head back into alignment with his neck and back. He went along with it all.

Despite my efforts, he still wore a slight frown; I then put my fingers at both sides of his mouth and pushed up to make a smile, but he refused to hold it in place. So I began telling a joke.

It was a joke about a man who played the bagpipes, a man lost on his way to play at the gravesite of a pauper's funeral. He eventually came across a few men on break from digging beside a large hole. It was so late that there was no one else around. The pastor and guests were probably long gone, so thought the piper, yet he began playing in earnest, and it was so heartfelt that everyone was led to tears. He felt great about his performance, and driving away, his heart was fulfilled. As he drove off, the men standing around holding shovels said, "I've never seen anything like that, and I've been putting in septic tanks for twenty years."

At that, the patient laughed and smiled. I asked him to hold that expression, and with his new, improved posture and outlook, I motioned for him to get off the table and move closer to the clinic room door.

"Now, go out just like that," I ordered. And he did.

On the way out of the clinic, he even gave the medical assistant the thumbs up. Later she told me that while she was checking him in, she'd told him that she felt sure that seeing me would help him; I suppose that had been his sign to her that she'd been right.

CHAPTER 4

Let the Heart Lead the Way

Toxic Exposure

A man with a full beard sat in the corner of the room. He was in his late forties with large, liquid brown eyes and the build of a football player. He was here after having had a physical and some bloodwork, as well as a full x-ray and a check of levels of possible chemicals in his blood measured. His employer had agreed to let him come and have a workup because he hadn't been feeling right over the course of the year at his job.

He told me that he handled chromium tetrafluoride, a coating for pipes that kept them from rusting. He handled the pipes with gloves on during his entire shift, though he'd felt the need to do some Internet-based research into his feelings of unwellness and tiredness that he thought were caused by the chromium. The articles he'd found named the culprit as toxic exposure to chemicals, one of which was the compound he handled daily. He also reported that he suffered from coughing, occasional nosebleeds, and fatigue that extended beyond what he felt after a hard day's work. He mentioned that he was scared that he was sick as a result of exposure to the chemical; however, the results of all of the exams and screenings had come back normal.

Coincidentally, I'd just seen two of his fellow employees from the same plant and assembly line as patients. Each had worked there for twenty-plus years with no health problems, and one had never even had a cold. They had come to see me for other reasons: one had been fitted with a new respirator, and the other had an injured foot mended. During those visits we'd talked at length about chromium and the safety standards of the plant as well as their own sense of safety. They had had no concerns, and so those discussions had given me great insight as I listened to the patient in front of me who had just started working there within the year.

I asked him to go further into his history, and he told me he was on a "shitload of medicines," from blood pressure to cholesterol to multiple oral medications for diabetes. He also mentioned that he had a very "hard row to hoe." When I asked him to tell me what he meant, he described the death of his father, mother, and wife, who died of an aneurysm, all within a year of each other, over the last several years. He was left broadsided and had begun eating very poorly, since his wife used to make home-cooked meals every day. He added that he felt as though he had a lot to live for, though his thirty-year-old daughter was always "riding his tail" to take better care of himself so he'd be alive for the grandchildren she wanted to share with him one day.

"Even without the need to do it for someone else, taking good care of yourself is a great idea, for your own sense of well-being," I said gently. "There never needs to be justification from any other person or future person to begin to do that."

He was a weary man who had lost his mojo, and life was wearing him down. He explained that he'd taken this job in the factory because he'd been let go from his previous job after twenty-seven years.

"You know, this year the percentage of people who are retiring with any intact pension or company-generated full benefits is only three percent. Companies can no longer afford to take care of their employees, which

Amy E. Coleman, MD

was the belief in the fifties and sixties. Today's economy is different," I told him.

I told him that anything can happen to us, and it's only what we choose to see that tints it as either good or bad. For example, you could lose a job and consider it as a blessing—the release from a nine-to-five prison. Someone else, however, could see this same event as the final nail in the coffin of his or her cursed life. It's the same event but perceived differently according to your state of mind.

I went further and told him that the same thing happened to my mom after twenty-three years on the job. She was let go just six months before retirement due to a sprained ankle that happened at work. The injury had been considered a negative impact on her productivity. As a result, for many years my mom suffered with that ankle, swollen and puffy and refusing to heal, because with each step she took, she was reminded of the hurt that she felt from being discarded after so many years of loyal service. Her feelings were hurt in the deepest way, and each twinge of pain reminded her of the betrayal, longing, and victimization she felt.

"We tend to personalize everything that happens to us," I explained. "We can see ourselves as victims of all that happens around us if we fall into an energy of feeling threatened and fearful. The whole world becomes a place that either has hurt us or will hurt us in some way."

I then told him that the death of his wife was not a loss. He could see it as a gain for heaven, and even for himself, because what he remembered of their relationship was the feeling of love for her, which was very much alive to that day, and always would be. Remembering shared events and kindling the nature of that heartfelt feeling of her would bring the same feeling back. She still existed, although not physically; instead of shutting out the feelings of her, he could then ask to invite them back in so she could always be with him. That is the glory of love—it's never lost unless we close our eyes to it.

I also shared the story of my father, who was an electrician and had once applied for a job at General Electric. Despite being three times more qualified than the other applicant, he wasn't hired because the company had to meet the quota of an equal-opportunity mandate that required them to hire, at that time, an individual who represented a minority race. That experience hurt my father's feelings so badly that he never went back to try out again and never extended himself in that way to any other job opportunity. My father, having seen himself as a victim of the event, still mentions the story to this day with some bitterness, even though it's been more than twenty years.

"Emotions are thoughts that carry intense currents of energy, such as the feeling of being wrapped in love," I went on. "It's a sense of warmth and peace—the highest energy you can feel. Now, in contrast, feelings of despair, guilt, shame, and fear bring a sense of cold, stabbing pain and isolation. When you think these thoughts long enough, you bathe your whole body in a climate of that energy."

I mentioned to the patient that the toxic exposure he was so concerned about had its source in his negative feelings thanks to all of the years of bitter feelings and noxious fumes of his perceived toils and struggles, which acted as a poison to his body's sense of wellness.

"This, over time, is more toxic than any chemical in the plant. You were not feeling well long before you started this job at the chemical plant. This has been many, many years of your life in the making," I declared.

"Wellness," I continued, "is a birthright. From two tiny cells, you became a perfectly formed person without having to take one medication. It's only when we get in the way of that natural flow that we generate the resistance and friction that the body has to then work around."

Since the patient had earlier shared with me that he found strength in Christianity, he and I joined for a prayer that went on for several minutes. After we opened our eyes, I sensed great peace and a resounding feeling of wellness in him.

"This feeling you have right now—it is your birthright. And the only thing that changed was the sequence of thoughts that changed your feelings, to change your whole perception of the world," I said.

He looked at me incredulously after a time of basking in the glow of the sweetness of the feeling and said, "I have always wanted to know, and always asked to know, why bad things happen to good people. I wish I had met you much earlier in my life. Things would have been different." I assured him that the timing was perfect as it was.

"You are so special," he said.

"You are too," I replied and embraced him in a large hug.

I felt so much love from this man. He was a transmission tower of the heart. I could only imagine the pain he'd experienced from locking this best part of himself away for so long, for fear of further injury to it. The warmth radiating from him was something I have truly remembered. The ember within him seemed like cold ash when he'd sat earlier alone in the corner, and after, he felt like a blazing bonfire.

Facelift

She was the next orange folder in the lineup of patients to see. An orange folder denotes an urgent care patient who has come to the clinic for a non-work-related injury or health complaint. When I'd opened her chart, there was plenty to see: ongoing headache, dizziness, multiple concussive head injuries, and anxiety.

The outer ego of me said, "Uggghhh," though my inner self reminded me that there was no order of difficulty in guiding someone to wellness.

When I stepped into the room, a pale young girl in her midthirties was sitting in the corner. Her expression was blank, though I saw fear and bewilderment in her eyes. She told me she was just trying out this clinic for a second opinion, since her doctor hadn't been listening to her and kept giving her more medications for her headache even though they hadn't been working. She went on to say that her symptoms had been worsening, and when she'd called her doctor over the phone to let him know, he'd been very critical and matter of fact. He accused her of not fully disclosing all of her symptoms in the last appointment. When she'd mentioned feeling a new symptom of dizziness, he'd snapped that the best he could do was provide a medication called meclizine, which might help the dizziness but would also make her sleepy.

In full interview mode, I then set about getting to know her: she worked as a paralegal and lived alone in Louisville with two dogs. Her mom also lived in Louisville, and they were close. Since she was young, she'd suffered from painful menstrual periods that had fully incapacitated her at the beginning of her cycle. She also had psoriasis and flaky, dry skin on her scalp and on small patches of her body. Her migraines, which used to be very bad as an adolescent but had subsided, had come back in full force in the last four months. She'd kept a journal to record triggers but had never been able to find any smells, foods, or menstrual cycle times that correlated with more headaches. She seemed to hit her head often and had suffered a concussion on several occasions though never experienced a loss of consciousness. She didn't drink but was a smoker and was also a vegetarian.

When I asked about her social life, she responded that she hadn't met the right guy yet. None were right for her, and at this statement, her energy went cold.

I then began a full, thorough physical examination, as I'd felt that gaining trust was essential before delving deeper. I noticed her stiff neck muscles, her flaky scalp, her light, rapid pulse, and her fine, petite frame with fair skin. Her neurological test was normal. Her thyroid was normal in size, but her muscles were a bit weak. I mentioned that to regulate her menstrual period and help with the headaches, she could use birth control pills. She acknowledged that but stated that her family history included a bleeding disorder, and since she smoked and was in her thirties, her physician had deemed her too high a risk for blood clots for the birth control pill. I then suggested that we could do some blood work to check her thyroid and for anemia as well as a neck x-ray to make sure that no harm was done after any of her several falls where she had hit her head in the past that may have been causing her headaches.

I then told her that we had only just dealt with the purely physical aspect of her care; there was a second leg to health, and that was the mental aspect. I asked her if she'd had any history of depression or anxiety. She told me that she was prescribed Xanax for many years due to panic attacks; however, she'd felt a deep need to be "normal" without medications and so weaned herself off. She was also on inhalers for asthma but found that she could also wean herself off of these when she noted that being anxious always led her to feeling tight chested, which preceded an asthma attack. She'd learned to divert her attention and practice self-calming techniques, such as deep breathing, to get through these difficulties.

I then began to see the real person behind the wall she'd initially placed when she'd first arrived. She had an amazing spirit and will to find her way past medications and learn that wellness was within her. I commended her for making this connection and told her that it took many pediatricians their whole lifetime of treating children to realize that asthma was very much related to anxiety. I told her what a strong person she was to seek past the answer that was offered to her by her doctor.

She'd mentioned that she hadn't wanted medications to be normal. I'd nodded my head in agreement. Most people want a quick fix and are happy to be given medications and be sent on their way. Most people don't want to delve so deeply into the source of their body's unrest and discontent. I mentioned that 99.9 percent or even more of doctors and patients accept this current model; however, true wellness is not about the medications.

I asked again about her relationships and whether she'd felt any stress or strain from that. She'd previously mentioned that she'd just broken off a relationship four months ago (when the migraines returned). I asked if she'd ever felt unsafe in a relationship. The answer was no. She denied any problems with any history of domestic abuse.

She'd been meeting and dating people she'd met online or through a dating site but felt as though they'd all been a waste of time. None of them had qualities she wanted; however, she'd also been concerned about her age (thirty-two years old) and that she'd spent a lot of time staying in her house or with her mom.

At this, I'd felt an incredible strain surfacing. She thought she'd be further along at this point in her life and then started to cry large sobs. She went on to say that she'd often refocus herself on her "puppies" at home and all the love they brought to her. She'd also remind herself to be thankful for the job she had. At this, I felt that her mind had talked herself into the blessings; since she'd identified such a void in relationships, she'd been walling off her true feelings with a, "Now, now, things aren't as bad as they seem" therapy, which at best had only temporarily capped the problem.

At that time it was important for her to know that the same situation that had caused her so much distress could be going on with someone else but with a completely different perception of the situation. I then began to tell her that I was thirty-seven and a half years old and also single with no children. I told her that I see it in a playful way, giving it to up to God to decide but not holding myself accountable for making it happen or judging myself harshly if it didn't. I shared with her how her harsh judgments on herself for not having found the right man and not having created the fruits of her expectations within her timeline had set up a very large resistance and discordance within her.

"You're like a pressure cooker or tiger pacing the cage," I told her. "This is enough to cause severe headaches and a sense of spinning out of control, which can manifest as dizziness. As sensitive as you are, your body is trying to talk to you. It wants to let you know that it's not happy in this emotional environment you have defined and is showing you in these signs and symptoms. Despite your best efforts to subdue and cap it with good feelings and walling off the problem, it's only adding more pressure. I wouldn't be surprised if you also had hemorrhoids."

"I do!" she replied in complete surprise.

She'd continued to cry since releasing the pent-up frustrations, and as a result, her face had shown more emotion and more personality. She smiled for the first time through her tears at some of the references in our discussion, and I'd seen her true self begin to emerge. I then introduced the third leg of health: spirituality. I asked if she had any association with meditation or faith of any kind. She answered that she was a Catholic and went to mass with her mother on Sundays. She liked to be in a church because the environment calmed her. I mentioned that she didn't have to go to church to feel that way—she could feel that way anywhere by identifying more with the God spark or soul within her.

For example, I explained that we draw to us our energetic equivalent; for her, this meant that she'd been drawing men to her that resulted in a sour experience for both parties. In her self-judgment of needing her life lined up in a certain way, she'd projected only judgment onto those she sought to attract; as a result, they'd judged her as well, with no room for love anywhere in that connection. I suggested that she might try a different approach. In first forgiving herself for what she felt was a failure in this department, she'd realize that with this forgiveness she could offer love and acceptance to herself and then offer it to all she'd meet.

More and more the color returned into her face and the fearful, dark eyes were replaced with vibrant ones. I'd told her how beautiful she was and how she was just now truly learning to embrace her sensitivities.

"They will be your greatest strength," I told her. "Your body will let you know when you are veering off course, like now. You are well and always have been."

She agreed, saying that she did feel well now.

"You're learning to listen to your own inner voice and are well on your path. You just needed a reminder that you have been believing in the wrong thoughts for a little too long, and they are not serving you."

I then asked if I could pray with her, and she grabbed both of my hands. I asked for her to be guided to any further wisdom that she needed and to be graced with assistance at every turn. I expressed my deep adoration and pure love for her and my true appreciation for her coming in and making my day.

As we concluded our visit, she hugged me with so much love. This had been a patient that had been pale and cold, with no perceptible emotion except fear when we first started. By the end, her whole countenance was rosy and glowing. She was quick to smile, and her eyes had a returned spark and inner radiance. It made my day that her true nature was back in place. I felt as much love for her as I had for anyone at any time in my life. I'd just spent a whole hour getting to know her, and so I gave her my card to reach me when needed. I also encouraged daily prayer or meditation and of course to stop smoking: the antithesis of her journey to health. She agreed.

How many golden lessons are we, as physicians, turning a blind eye to, simply because patients are coming in their time of greatest need, projecting their worst selves outwardly at the time of their visit? How many sages are behind the mask they initially present? These patients need only a gentle nudge and a simple reminder that they are indeed *still* that same wise person but have temporarily misplaced their focus to identify more with the turmoil and unbalance, which they have come to despise. My highest intention is not to agree with the illusion that they have mistakenly embraced but to redirect them to their true nature. It is to fully embrace love, from which they were created.

Canary in a Coal Mine

The next patient was an attractive, fit lady in her mid-thirties who, by appearance, had taken good care of herself. She'd come to the clinic for a refill of her carbamazepine that she used to control her trigeminal neuralgia, which had begun to flare up again. She'd completed all levels of therapy, including surgical decompression therapy and ablative surgery and had taken many different medications, including Neurontin, and a brief course of pain medication, which hadn't worked. She explained that after much investigation on her own, she'd noticed that excess sugar seemed to worsen the problem.

"I cut out sugar," she said, "and noticed that this has helped a lot. But I just got back from a cruise and so am trying to get back on my routine."

"It's great that you found the connection between sugar and your outbreaks," I said. "Something else that could cause an exacerbation in symptoms is stress. Have you had much stress lately?"

She'd nodded her head with eyes wide open.

"The reason that stress is such an irritant is because many of us hold tension in our mouths and jaws, which is exactly where the affected nerve is in trigeminal neuralgia sufferers. As a matter of fact, we go to bed with the same amount of tension that we carry during the day, which continues throughout the night. By the time we wake up, our muscles have been working all night long to maintain this flexion. Just try holding your arm up in front of you, and see how long you can do this before you feel like your arm is going to fall off.

"This is why sleep hygiene is so important," I went on. "Having a warm bath in soaking salts, lighting a candle, having some quiet time to unwind with a book, scripture, deep breathing, prayer, or meditation, unwinds the day. Not doing so puts our poor bodies in a sort of Chinese water torture. We may clench our jaws, flexing our mouth and jaw muscles, which, after a night of sleep like this, can cause the fatigued muscle to spasm in exhaustion. The muscle that's now hard as concrete irritates the neighboring nerve, and so shooting nerve pain begins from the now-agitated nerve. It's a vicious cycle."

I then suggested she try a mild muscle relaxant at night for a short period to help to break the cycle. She mentioned that she sometimes reads the scripture to relax, but since she'd returned from her vacation, she'd felt a need to catch up at work and with home projects. She mentioned that she loved Jesus, and I agreed outright and smiled, feeling warmth in my heart.

"Stress is the time when it is most important to continue your nightly scripture regimen," I went on. "For, in a whole day, we become too much wrapped up in the world around us. A wise man said to be *in* the world, but not *of* the world."

I continued to explain to her that science was even coming to know the perfection of these higher quality emotions and thoughts through new fields of physics that explain everything I discussed in terms of vibration levels. We all are energy at our core, and shifts in our focus of thought can change the energy we maintain around us. When we identify with lower-quality vibrations, such as emotions or thoughts, we bathe the surrounding cells of our body in a broth that isn't consistent with health. Eventually, the body *will* manifest a disease or state of unwellness, as its job is to translate the climate of the mind over time.

"In a way, your trigeminal neuralgia is a blessing, not a curse," I stated. "It's your canary in a coal mine, so to speak. It's the first thing to complain when you're the least bit off your path. When your stress level goes up, or when you stop nurturing your body, such as choosing the wrong foods for too long, it will remind you to come back to your center. It's your wake-up call.

"So when it begins to become painful, consider it a reminder for you to reassess where you are in your walk of faith, as your body is feeling the tug of strain that goes inevitably along with the mind taking on too much on its own," I finished.

"I feel so connected with you right now," she said. "I've had a physician who was a Christian, but I have never met anyone like you who is such an example and teacher of it. I wasn't even going to come today, but something said that I should."

"I've had other patients tell me that," I said, "and I believe they are brought in to hear what they need and are ready to hear. I thought briefly about going to school to become a pastor, but people need to know how connected the spirit is to our true physical health, and I help them make that connection. The connection you said that you feel is what we are supposed to feel and experience when any one of our brothers or sisters of humankind sits across from us. It is always an opportunity to share a special, heartfelt bond.

"How do you feel, for example, when a physician enters the room with his/ her nose in a computer, not even looking up to make eye contact, with a sense of hurry in his or her voice, cutting off your sentences and rushing the exam?" I continued. "That physician is demonstrating the example of what we become when we become overidentified with our minds, and the result is how the mind typically does business."

I then thanked her for her visit. We hugged warmly, and she asked me to let her know when I opened a clinic in the area.

Calling All Angels

I heard her speaking from the room where the nurse was measuring her vitals before her visit with me. I couldn't make out the entire conversation but caught a few words here and there. Most were spoken in a soft tone: "I've been through a lot … it's been horrible … I just feel depressed." The voice, though soft, was strong and knowing.

When the medical technician brought her to the exam room, I was taken aback by the incredibly large, dark circles under her eyes and how she was able to walk so erect despite having the distinct upper back hump of osteoporosis. Her hair was gray, and her face had layers of wrinkles, not just in lines but lines on top of lines, forming a wrinkle grid. She had bright blue eyes and began speaking immediately of more serious concerns, although she'd been checked in chiefly due to the complaint of a cough.

She'd been the sole caretaker of her aging mother (who had recently passed), along with holding down a full-time job and living alone, managing the home and upkeep since her divorce. Although she had thirteen siblings, many were into drugs and alcohol, and she, the oldest, had always been the most reliable. She went on further to tell me that for the last couple of months, she'd had a new boss who'd been trying to prove himself by micromanaging everyone with a critical eye. Though she was the only woman in a group of twenty-five men, she'd never been made to feel uncomfortable until the boss's new attention to detail; it made her feel scrutinized and inadequate. She'd even confronted the new boss on a few occasions, which had left her feeling ill at ease.

I asked her to transition from the chair to the examining room table as she continued on with her story.

She told me that she was a God-fearing woman and so had made sure she encouraged her fellow workers to watch their tongues and not swear, at least around her. She showed me how she did this: while holding her index finger up to her mouth and looking them square in the eyes, she'd tell them not to be a potty mouth, but then always made sure to tell them that, "it's okay, God loves you just as much as He loves me." She felt that her corrections were never out of meanness or judgment but as an attempt to create a better environment around her.

At yearly business parties, she felt uncomfortable with the alcohol consumption and so would stay a little while and then make her rounds to a say good-bye. As she was leaving, she would make sure she prayed that God help them all. I praised her for holding firm for her beliefs and for sending good will to others when she herself was in an uncomfortable situation.

I then got back to the situation with her boss. "Thoughts are very powerful," I said. "They attract more thoughts similar to themselves all the time, just like a group of friends at school. The troublemakers attract more troublemakers to themselves, and a small clique enlarges to a gang, and on to a posse. So choose your thoughts like you choose your friends, because they will multiply. So, you'd better like the company you'll be keeping!"

I also mentioned that when someone is put into a higher level of responsibility, it often brings out fear and insecurity in the person, which can bring to the surface these weaknesses.

"When you focus on the insecurities in a person," I explained, "you amplify it for them. That sweet person you saw before fades to the background even more as they become more identified with the part of them that they most likely despise in themselves as well. Their fellow colleague calling it out and recognizing this small part of their character, now taking center stage in the daily business, further magnifies this. It's our job to recognize our brother with love and not judgment," I finished.

In response she told me that she'd noticed having a shorter fuse since her mother's death, which had left her feeling so exhausted from caring for her for so long. She resented that she was sent right back to work after the funeral, as she felt she needed some time to grieve. She began crying more at this.

"Grief can last two to six months, and it's normal to feel as though you cannot function for quite a while after a loved one's death," I told her gently, offering her some tissues.

When I asked her if she ever felt the presence of her mother, she said, "You're going to think I'm crazy, but I seem to hear her as a voice inside my head. Then when I ask her questions, it's almost as though she's answering me," the patient replied.

"You are not crazy," I said, supporting her with a hand on her knee. "There have been lots of studies regarding the body when it dies, and there is a weight that lifts at the time of death, thought to be due to the presence of the soul. The soul is what is alive, not the bag of skin and clothes that we wear around. I wouldn't be talking to you if you were just the luggage of your body sitting on the table. I wouldn't even consider you alive unless your soul was intact, so truly, *that* is the part that makes you alive. Quite honestly, your mother is just as alive now as she was when she was wearing a body around, because the soul does, and always will, exist."

The patient went on to tell how strange it was to hear in her mind communication that she did not see leave someone's physical lips in front of her. I went on to say that this was explained by instances when a mother seems to just know what is going on with her children without them having to tell her.

"Communication doesn't have to be from the mouth," I continued. "Communication exists at all times when we have ties of love with someone else. There have been studies to prove this as well, even at the smallest sizes of life. For example, when two protons are placed together for an extended amount of time and are then removed from each other and separated by long distances, the distances don't seem to matter at all. The changing of one proton, wherever it is, causes the other proton to change as well, at the same time! This is called empathy to us and entanglement by science. Whether in a scientific sense or a relationship sense, there are real, unseen ties that bind us all."

The patient nodded in agreement, even telling funny incidents of when her mother called out her naughty siblings without anyone tattling. There was a running joke among the children that "she always knows." At this, I let her know that there was no reason why she could not continue to embrace the spirit of her mother, keeping her engaged in her daily life.

She went on to say that when she needs guidance, she often sits with her hand on the Bible that her mother gave her, closes her eyes, and asks, "What would you do, Mom?" At this, she relates that if she waits and is still for a moment, she gets an answer in her ear.

As she said this, I noticed a beautiful light just over the patient's head, elevated about six to eight inches over her, that beamed and then quietly dimmed and vanished. I thanked the light internally for allowing me to help this woman who needed to know she was not alone.

"She is just as alive, even more so than you or me," I told her softly. "In this form she can always be with you when you think of her. But when you choose the thoughts of sadness and loneliness, you choose, in effect, to block her out. You stare straight ahead, almost with blinders on to anyone or anything that could cheer you, because you've chosen to see, ironically, what is false, that you're alone and without her. When you have conversations with her, asking her questions and keeping close the things that were dear to her, you open the door to allowing her in your life."

The patient nodded in agreement and wiped her eyes and her nose, which at that point were quite red from crying so much. I then turned to a different subject, which had been the main reason she'd come in: her cough. We discussed an antibiotic to use for her chronic bronchitis due to smoking and a prescription for an inhaler, as well as a strong cough syrup. I also gave her a refill of her osteoporosis medication.

When I asked her about stopping smoking, she said that she'd tried many things, but always fell right back into the habit when her stress became out of control. I mentioned a medication called Wellbutrin that helps to lessen the cravings for cigarettes, giving her a firmer emotional platform on which to stand since her symptoms of depression and grief had been peaking in the last several months. I told her that this medication helps with both kicking the nicotine habit and depression. In response she stated that she'd been on this medication before and thought she'd remembered experiencing a positive effect.

I reminded her that the medication was not a miracle pill that would keep her from smoking. She had to do her part as well. At that she mentioned a prayer she'd been using for many months: that God would help her to stop smoking. She stated that after all that praying, she'd received an answer in return. That answer had been, "I delivered you from these cigarettes long ago, but you must do your part!" She said that this made her feel inadequate.

"I am just so stupid," she said emphatically.

I then held up my ten fingers and stated, "Most people have the same ten thoughts every day. When it comes to how they feel about themselves, it's an old rerun that continues over and over. How many thoughts of yourself during the day, of these top ten, are positive?"

At this, she shook her head and said, "Zero."

I reminded her that humility is a virtue, but confidence allows us to serve others, and ourselves, better.

"As women, we are often raised not to take any credit for things and to keep serving others until we collapse from exhaustion," I stated. "With this type of programming, we often do not develop very good self-esteem. As a result, we fail others and ourselves because we are not firmly rooted with love for ourselves. In its place, feelings of inferiority take root, which cause us to reach toward external sources of strength to patch what we feel we don't have inside of ourselves to do. That may be cigarettes for some, alcohol for others, or promiscuity for someone else. It's all in an attempt to find that something that gives us what we feel we are missing. Feelings of inadequacy continue this ineffective programming."

Then I pointed out something that surprised her. "God works in sometimes humorous ways. Now that we're thinking with positive thoughts and able to see the situation from a bit more of a bird's-eye view, rather than down in the dumps, you need to know that there is a reason why people are attracted into your life. Each one is a lesson for us. Each one reflects to us something we need to know about ourselves. Your new boss, as irritating and intimidating and irrational as you say he is, and as much as everyone else agrees, do you know what you two have in common?" I asked.

She looked puzzled.

"The answer is that you both share strong feelings of inadequecy." God knows that the help you need the most to stop smoking is to get over your feeling of inadequacy so you can find the inner strength to kick cigarettes to the curb for good; God puts someone in front of you every day who also has the same insecure feelings so you will finally realize that this way of thinking does you, and everyone else, no good. His hope is that you'll see the lesson in this relationship. This boss is a noble friend, not an enemy. What irritates us the most about others is what reminds us of the parts of ourselves we don't like. That's why you aren't just a little annoyed but very angry and even confrontational about his behavior. It reminds you of the inadequacy in yourself!" I finished emphatically.

At this she tilted her head, trying to understand. "I never thought of it that way," she said. "I was very hard on him recently, and I was going to go back later and tell him that it was because I cared for him and didn't want him to fail, but I never went back."

"It would never be too late to tell him that," I replied. "You can always see things from a higher perspective if you clear out the negative talk and the feelings of being a victim of a situation. If you look at everything that happens to you as a potential lesson, you will begin to see why and how things happen the way they do. You were not the oldest of thirteen to work away in a life of feudal slavery. You were put there because you were the strongest of them all, but you have never seen that for yourself. There is a quote from the Bible: 'Much is given to one from whom much is expected.' He gifted you with strength, courage, and fortitude. You are the only woman of twenty-five men in your working environment, and you manage your own home by yourself. You took care of your mom. You have strength beyond measure. You walk in faith every day with more dedication to applying your faith to your actions than anyone I have ever seen. So you receive all the help you need from above to accomplish any mission. But you choose to see it another way, from a state of loss and woulda, shoulda, coulda. God just wants you to see what he sees, and he is trying so hard to bring that into your awareness. That is why you are here today."

"Yes, it is," she agreed. "I wasn't even going to stop here today, because I'm going to see my regular doctor of twenty-seven years next week. But something told me to come."

"What you see is always a choice," I reminded her.

"I feel like so much is coming out now," she said. "There is something else really bothering me now. My son would've been forty-five this coming month," she said, hanging her head very low. "I dread that time of being without him."

At this, I had her remember that, just as she was in contact with her mother, she could be in contact with her son as well if she would open up to the idea of it. In that light, the anniversary would be more like a homecoming than another funeral. I saw a flint of hope in her eye as she looked up again.

"You are such a blessing to me," I said. "I see thousands of patients, and you are one of the strongest, most capable souls I have ever met. You remind me to ask for help from God for everything. Those men at work don't even think to ask if you need time off or help because you look so capable at doing anything!"

"Yes, they often watch me do jobs they even have a hard time doing, and I think they may be a little jealous," she replied.

"No," I said, firmly. "They're just thinking that they wish they could do it half as good as you when they reach your age. You are a great example to so many people."

I then felt her spirit lift at the thought that someone recognized her for what she *truly* was. I asked her if I could pray with her, and she held both my hands and bowed her head. Afterward we hugged, and I walked her to the front desk to check her out and offer her a well-deserved two-day hiatus from work for her terrible cough. I hugged her again and then reminded her to follow up with me in a month.

On her way out to go to the pharmacy and fill her prescriptions, she said, "You can call me anytime, even at work!"

This patient truly demonstrated how the bond of love we form with a mother or loved one—that allows that person to know how we are and to share love—is not interrupted when we pass from the physical to the light. It is just on a more subtle frequency. There is no time or distance between love; love is what reveals the illusory effect of both.

Heart to Heart

The patient I was to see next was a forty-six-year-old white male with a history of heart problems. He'd had an open-heart bypass and a pacemaker/defibrillator placed years previously. When I walked into the room, he was sitting slumped over his clipboard, which was filled with notes he was taking about his job while he waited. He had a whipped-dog look in his eyes—a whipped dog that had been beaten down for a very long time and was in a state of resignation.

When I looked at his EKG, there were anomalies on it called Q waves and other electrical abnormalities that suggested scarring from an old heart attack. He began telling me his fascinating story, which mesmerized me. He had grown up as an athletic runner and never had any health problems. Later, he became a commercial pilot and enjoyed his job very much. However, at a yearly physical, it was noted that he had some abnormal beats on his EKG. After he saw a cardiologist, doctors decided to perform a cardiac catheterization, which involved introducing a catheter into the groin at the femoral vein for access into the heart, in order to visualize the coronary arteries.

With radiological dye to illuminate the heart vessels, his cardiologist found a misdirected coronary artery, which passed between the aorta and pulmonary vessel. This was unknown territory for the normal path of a coronary artery, he was told. In times of exercise, his doctor postulated that this vessel became squeezed, and over time, the part of the heart that received only partial circulation from this crimped blood vessel became scarred. These areas, his doctor had explained, were less likely to conduct normal heart rhythms and were more resistant to flowing in harmony with the natural electronic current conducted by other areas of the heart. Electrical charges in the scarred portion could become stagnant and result in storms of electricity, which led to irregular beats and rhythms.

Not surprisingly, a heart bypass surgery was recommended by harvesting and using a vessel in the leg to replace the coronary artery. This new vessel would supply the scarred side of the heart with better circulation. However, the surgery was not successful. The heart continued to go into storms of electrical activity, reaching rates as high as three hundred beats per minute. During these events, the patient would go into ventricular tachycardia, a life-threatening arrhythmia. After multiple episodes of this, the patient then had a defibrillator placed, which shocked him each time the abnormal arrhythmia happened. An internal defibrillator shock would feel very similar to the kind used in emergency rooms when a patient becomes unresponsive on the table and must be brought to life with charged paddles on his or her chest. Hundreds of joules of energy are triggered instantaneously to confuse and reset the rhythm of a waywardly bounding heart.

With this defibrillator placed inside his chest, the patient reported that on one memorable occasion, it shocked him six times before the EMTs arrived at his house to take him to the hospital. He never lost consciousness during these multiple electrical assaults, except for when he stood up to be led to the stretcher, at which time he passed out.

The emotional toll of these experiences left him feeling so frightened that he would not leave the house. He became scared to go out. The moment he thought about the defibrillator going off, the fear caused his heart to race, and then he would become even more fearful that the rhythm would go out of sync again as a result. Thankfully, he received help from an electrophysiologist, who plotted the electrical conductance of his heart and was able to use a laser to eradicate the short-circuiting areas that perpetuated the heart in its uncontrollable gallop. After several treatments, the patient noticed that he wasn't being shocked anymore. The heart did enter into an irritable rhythm only once after the procedure, but the pacemaker device within the defibrillator was able to wave this off, settling the heart rhythm again without requiring a shock.

"Do you still experience the same anxiety as when you were having the shocks and frequent heart arrhythmias, or have you been able to relax now that it had been repaired?" I asked, interested to know how he unwound the spiral of tension and anxiety that had been programmed from the torturous cardiac events.

He mentioned that although the incidences of shocking had stopped, he still suffered from severe anxiety and depression. He was trying to come to terms with the fact that he would no longer be able to do the things he enjoyed and that living with possible occasional shocks and arrhythmias were his fate. He used mental counseling and talk therapy, as well as antidepressants and valium daily. He mentioned that he used to love to run six miles a day, but now he felt that he should not have "abused" his body in this way. I told him that there is no blame, guilt, or shame in exercising a body and that he was actually doing the right thing for his health by staying active and healthy. I encouraged him to let go of the belief that he caused his heart problems. This repetitive idea of self-blame was causing him only more desperation.

"We all have a cross to bear, don't we?" I began. "We all have our allotted tests in life. But can I ask you something? Have you learned to see the lesson in this for you yet, or are you still looking at it from a purely mechanical standpoint?" He looked at me questioningly.

"You have two parts to your brain," I began. "One part is purely mathematical and logical, using physical evidence as the source of all answers. The other side is purely creative and abstract—but is just as important. Both sides of the brain need to be in balance. However, for some of us, we develop one side predominantly and come to rely on it much more than the other side. This is when we become unbalanced. When we become more concrete, logical, and purely mathematically focused, we become less flexible in our views and allow for less of what is felt, inspired, and intuited. Rather, we remain rigid in what we can measure and what the calibrated instruments around us reflect. It becomes an existence of contrived control of the mind, by the mind. The other side of your brain desperately wishes to be known by you.

"This more abstract part of the brain allows us to realize something very important, and that is that we are more than just a brain and our three-dimensional existence. We are much more multifaceted. Even science has proven that there are more dimensions of space and time than we can currently measure. These dimensions exist but are unseen and are proving to be governed by laws of science just now being realized by scientists." With this, I introduced the higher dimensional aspect of the soul.

"Do you believe that you have a soul?"

"Yes," he stated assuredly.

"That part of you wants to be so much a part of your life, but it cannot exist through the black-and-white, logical framework that you have created in which to see your world. Your mind is the problem, trying to make sense of its own predicament.

"You need a more aerial view of the terrain, just as you did when you were a pilot flying, able to look down and see the big picture below. The mind and body can only see from the ground level, lost among the weeds and unable to see their way out of the maze. The soul gives this aerial view. You need only to hold the intention of knowing this part of yourself more fully to activate it into your awareness. It does not take an organized religion or a priest. We all have what it takes within us to know this part of ourselves. It is the universal, unified source that we all share. We are all like streetcars, attached to the same overhead electric cables, omniscient, and all-knowing power stations that we can tap into at any time.

"I have felt what your way feels like, and it is painful. As you were telling your story, I shared in your feelings; my chest was tight and felt bound up, pulling into the center, and painful. I could not even take a deep breath. My stomach felt upset and worried. I would not stand to live a day like that," I admitted.

"How do you like the way you feel now? You are hearing my story, how I govern myself and my beliefs about the world. So you are sharing the feelings that go with that now. It is soul speak. This is not a conversation with the mind. It is one from the heart and soul." As I looked at him, I could feel and see how comfortable he had become. I was so in tune with his feelings at the time that my own level of relaxation had passed directly and instantaneously to him.

"You don't have the chest pain anymore, and you are truly relaxed." The patient took a deep breath. "See, you can even breathe deeply. I bet it has been a while since you could do that." I felt the deliciousness of this feeling for him, almost as a starving man finding food again, and it reminded me to be thankful of the blessing that I have every day to breathe deeply. "The most important thing to realize is that you can choose which way you would like for your life to feel—your way or this way."

"I like this way," he said, wide-eyed and incredulous. I sensed he did not want to move or speak so that he could enjoy the refreshment.

"Now, what you are feeling is what it feels like to be close to the truth that is you. You are spirit, a ghost surrounded by skin, with connections to a much larger existence. But when you ignore that part of yourself, the farther you get away from this truth, the more miserable you will feel. You will become anxious and depressed and wonder if this life is as good as it gets. As you tinker with getting everything in place the way it logically makes sense, you will never get it 'just right.' This is because your mind was never meant to take on so much and because the physical world is always in shift. The mind was supposed to be the daily manager of what is right in front of you. It is not meant to take on the visionary, long-range planning of your life and events that are outside of your control. We all inherently know that there is a deeper wisdom to what appears on the surface of the life in front of us. But you don't need to be a ninety-year-old person to have this wisdom. You can find that for yourself now."

"But how do I get there from here?" he questioned.

"You hold the intention in a quiet place of meditation to know this part of yourself," I said. "The fact that I am here talking to you about this today means that you have already been considering it, so it is already happening, although you think you are far from it. To be honest, whenever you have a question, the answer is already in front of you. You must have access to the answer if you can think of the question at all. In accessing this moment in a quiet place, you contact the unified field: God, Buddha, Jesus, your highest self. It is all the same.

"So if you like the feeling that you are experiencing, choose it over the old feeling that you had. It is a similar process when you find a new favorite food. You figure out the ingredients, you talk to a chef to learn how to make it, you buy the ingredients, all from the simple intention of your choice to have it more often. You will experience in your daily life something that grabs your attention, to direct you closer to the next thing you need to know and the next step you need to take. Just trust it is the next guidance you need—just like this visit. Nothing happens just by coincidence."

At that, the clipboard that he had guarded under his right thigh during our visit had become wedged out from his leg and unbalanced, and it fell to the floor. "That is exactly where that belongs now," I said.

"You had to go through the health problems you did to break down your stubborn will far enough so you would reach for a different solution. Obviously, your way is not working. It feels miserable, and I can attest to that by sharing it with you today. Empathy allows us to truly feel what others are feeling, if we truly care, relax, and listen. It is good that we could share each other's perspective, and that is all it is. I used no procedure, device, or medicine to change you during the time of our visit, and yet you feel peace. It was all a shift of your perception that allowed just a little ray of light in, so that you could remember what the truth feels like."

As I left, I said, "You are more than welcome to use this room for a while and just sit, enjoy, relax, or reflect—whatever you would like to do, for as long as you would like."

"I would like to stay here for a moment," he said with appreciation and a countenance of hope.

This patient encounter was so powerful for me. In experiencing fully this patient's perspective through deep listening, I had traveled virtually with him through his story. It was as if I allowed myself to fully feel what he was feeling, and as a result of that pure intention of connection, I was then able to choose to reconnect to the preferred energy that I know as my truth. By intending to return to my baseline calm state, he was carried with me into that space, which was a new experience for him. I felt him relax and experience what has become for me my best self: a state of being relaxed, at peace, loved, warmed, and nurtured. His taste of experiencing renewal this way was sheer bliss, not only for him but for me as well. It was like sharing ice cream or sunshine with someone who had only lived in a land with no sweets and only rain.

Footnote: A Lesson in "What You Give, You Get."

Later after clinic that evening, I described the whole scenario and scene of this patient encounter to my fiancé. I realized that this type of medicine was what I was truly meant to do: to reflect the light that each one of us has and amplify it so that others can get in touch with it themselves. So often we allow someone in poor spirits to draw our attention into his or her contagious energy, and we stay there with that person, trapped in the quicksand of his or her circumstance and bad feelings. Within this scenario, no one is helped. Two people in misery do not solve any problem.

I was learning that through prayer, mindfulness, and deep listening, I could be truly present for a patient. I could "try on," so to speak, the depth of their despair and feel it for myself. Then, after a time, in the same spirit of empathy, I could return to my baseline level of love, peace, and joy. In that moment of shared empathy, patients are carried with me to my own sense of well-being, and they remember the possibility of this for themselves. I felt my heart and joy could never be more full. I felt that this was what I was born to do.

Sitting on the couch a home, I looked at the painting across the room I had painted of a show-jumping horse and rider. A beautiful realization came over me. With my head in my hands, I began to cry as I gently realized that the sport of show jumping had always been only a physical interpretation of my dream of being airborne and soaring high in partnership. It was a lifelong passionate dream of mine, and this horse sport was the earth-bound translation of that concept. Ironically, in looking at my painting, I realized that show jumping could never come close to the loftiness of spirit and aerial view that I had experienced that day with my patient. God indeed had been out to show me that I was meant for more than I could ever imagine. I was allowed a glimpse of what true flying was about. It was about experiencing my spirit soaring to heights I had never known. Show jumping could never dream of reaching the magnitude of this dynamic potential. I cried with relief from the frustration and years of judgment on myself for not having reached my equestrian show-jumping goals. I could never understand why there seemed to be an obstacle for me to advance in the sport. My competitive-riding dreams always competed with and were shadowed by the demanding environment of medicine. I had wondered why this goal I had since I was a child was not made manifest, when all my other dreams and goals had been so easily reached. The answer was now right in front of me. I was to know more heights than physical jumps could ever be set. Aligned with God and His purpose for me, this was only now being made known to me in a way that I truly understood.

The relief spread through me like a wave of peace, and I was finally able to take a deep breath. This breath was a release of years of judgment on myself in the sport. Now I saw that I was officially out of my own way, as the goal had already been in reach the whole time and was bigger and better than I could have imagined. Show jumping was just dessert, something to be enjoyed for the sheer love of the connection with an animal and love of sport. I had no other ambition for it with this new realization; all resistance at this moment was severed at its core source.

I was finally able to enjoy that first deep breath and profound peace that release to higher wisdom and alignment brings, just as my patient had experienced earlier in the day. I was reaping what I had sown and receiving what I had given. The sense of wonderment in this was beyond my brain to comprehend, but ironically, my heart understood it all.

ABOUT THE AUTHOR

Dr. Amy Coleman originally served as a United States Air Force Flight Surgeon after medical school and internship, where she was appointed as the youngest and first female Commander of the U.S. Air Force Special Operations Clinic. There, she helped guide global medical missions and built creative clinic systems including those employing complementary care methods still in operation today throughout the U.S. Air Force. Sought out for her "mind, body and spirit approach to patient care, she was selected as the primary physician for Four-Star Generals, U.S. Embassies, Special Forces Teams, F-16 Fighter Squadrons and was a contracted Flight Surgeon to NASA for Space Shuttle support missions. She also served in Iraq during Operation Iraqi Freedom. Dr. Coleman trained as a Family Medicine physician at University of Kentucky and is certified in Japanese Acupuncture from Harvard. Currently, Dr. Coleman is CEO and Founder of Wellsmart, a company which cultivates technologies and healthcare strategies that strengthen the patient/doctor relationship.

ABOUT THE COVER

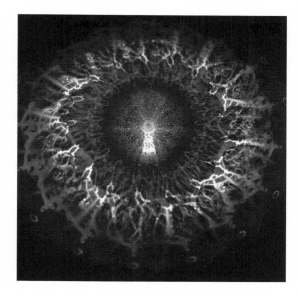

The cover design image is created from fractal mathematic algorithms. Fractals are laws of nature explained in mathematical form. In science, fractals are used to study the harmony within biological systems.

The picture of the iris of an eye with a keyhole in the center represents the deeper meaning of "Discovering Your Own Doctor Within." These stories remind us that answers are found by going within to consult our higher conscious awareness.

This image was brought to life by commissioned artist Kapil Bambardekar, from Mumbai, India. (www.sleeplessmonk.com) A PhD in biophysics with experience in microscopy, scientific image processing and art therapy, Kapil applied his knowledge of fractal mathematics and code art to generate the cover design.

Kapil calls himself a humble explorer of reality. His artistic vision is to "create moments of non-duality: pockets beyond time and space to provide a pathway for uninhabited exploration. A tool for people to discover themselves and live fully their unique vision of reality hidden dormant within."